Mother O' Mine

A Legacy of Remembrance

Harry W. Paige

Resurrection Press
An Imprint of
CATHOLIC BOOK PUBLISHING CO.
Totowa • New Jersey

First published in September 2003 by
Catholic Book Publishing/Resurrection Press
77 West End Road
Totowa, NJ 07512

ISBN 1-878718-81-9
Library of Congress Catalog Card Number: 2003104518

Cover design by Beth DeNapoli
Cover photo enhanced by Faye A. Serio

Printed in the United States of America

1 2 3 4 5 6 7 8 9 10

When the author was in fourth grade he wrote a prize-winning composition. The prize was a book inscribed by the teacher and the boy ran home after school to show his mother.

"That's a handsome prize," she praised, examining the book. And then she added with an encouraging smile: "Maybe you'll be a writer when you grow up."

"If I am a writer then I'll write a book for you," the boy said.

And a promise is a promise.

In memory of my mother
RUTH A. PAIGE

Note from the editor:

On September 13, 2003 Harry Paige joined his beloved mother in eternity. We join them in celebrating the keeping of his promise to her.

OTHER BOOKS BY HARRY W. PAIGE

Contents

Part III: The Long Good-bye 113

MOTHER O' MINE

If I were hanged on the highest hill,
    Mother o' mine, o mother o' mine!
I know whose love would follow me still,
    Mother o' mine, o mother o' mine!
If I were drowned in the deepest sea,
    Mother o' mine, o mother o' mine!
I know whose tears would come down to me,
    Mother o' mine, o mother o' mine!
If I were damned by body and soul,
    Mother o' mine, o mother o' mine!
I know whose prayers would make me whole,
    Mother o' mine, o mother o' mine!

— Rudyard Kipling

"And I saw in the turning so clearly a child's
Forgotten mornings when he walked with his mother
    Through the parables
        Of sun light
And the legends of the green chapels
And the twice told fields of infancy . . ."

— Dylan Thomas
"Poem in October"
in *Collected Poems*,
New Directions

Acknowledgements

ACKNOWLEDGEMENT is gratefully extended to the following for permission to include here essays originally published elsewhere:

THE CATHOLIC DIGEST

"My Mother's Mother," first published under the title "How To Make Things Holy," July, 2002.

"Mother's Book of Hope," first published in August, 1994.

"A Family's Paper Trail," first published in June, 1997.

"Echoes of a Lost Sunday," first published in February, 1997.

"Ringing Home," first published in May, 1996.

"Mother's Shooting Star," first published in August, 1996.

LIGUORIAN

"A Tale of Two Churches," first published in September, 2000.

"A Mother's Song," first published in December, 1996.

"Beacons of Light," first published in February, 2002.

"Lost and the Miracle of Being Found," first published in July, 1998.

"From Mourning Into Morning," first published in May, 1998.

"A Lifetime of Words, an Eternity of Silence," first published in November, 1999.

"An Eternal Reunion," first published in November, 1997.

ROUNDUP MAGAZINE, a publication of the Western Writers of America.

"A Surrogate Son," first published under the title "Death Song," August, 2000.

The author would also like to thank the following people for their assistance in the writing of this book:

My sister, Jeanne P. Adams of Manchester, Connecticut for sharing a part of her life and memories with me,

The Adams family for their memories,

My own daughters, Judith and Sandy, for their remembrances of things past,

And Emilie Cerar, of Resurrection Press for her thoughtful direction.

Preface

I BEGIN my journey of remembrance with my mother's leaving on February 17, 1996, for that is the way memory works—from endings to beginnings, from death to life. Memory is a resurrection on the human level as well as a divine promise. And, although I now leave her to heaven, as she would have wished, I do lay claim to her memory, especially to those *shared* memories that often follow death like bright shadows of solace and redemption.

When I think of mother I think of *home*, a home she spun, spider-like from deep within. I think of a house of breath, a house of love. Not a *place* so much as a way and an aura . . .

A lover of things as they were, my mother will never be remembered as a housekeeper: she loved a sweet disorder of her own creation. She loved antiques, dust and the musty odors of time. She loved the delicate pattern of cobwebs that festooned the ceiling and wafted from the corners of things. They were, to her, memories made visible. Flimsy and gauzy they were not only reminders of neglect, but also of endurance and patience. They moved to the prevailing currents of draft and breath like fragile signals from yesterday.

"Cobwebs are stronger than steel," she told me more than once, not so much as an excuse for not brooming them down as an explanation for their preservation.

Cobwebs are stronger than steel!

Characteristically, she never explained her words. She left them hanging, a paradox on the sill of reflection. Perhaps her words were a cryptic statement about the past and its constant intrusions on the present. Perhaps a measure of the strength of memory. Perhaps a mystery not to be solved but to be celebrated. Perhaps words to make my sister and I see cobwebs in a different way, not so much as evidence of neglect or laziness but as time's art, a tapestry of yesterday.

11

I remember especially the only home our family owned, the home she lived in and loved for almost sixty years. The mother of homes! Today strangers occupy it and when I visit my hometown I drive by slowly for a look-see. It is re-modeled now, brought up to date for the new millennium. The leaning birches and crooked maples are gone from the front yard, allowing a flood of sunshine to nourish the new lawn. The driveway has been re-surfaced, covering the cracks from which aberrant yet persistent flowers sprung. The natural look of the backyard ("Mother's Wilderness", we called it) is gone in favor of neat, geometric patterns. The dogwood, planted by the wind and nourished by hope, has been uprooted. The woods that filled the adjacent lot has disappeared and a house now stands there. The flowers that bordered and sometimes overhung the driveway are gone. The sundial I made no longer translates sunshine and shade into hours and minutes. All gone!

After the take-over by well-intentioned strangers I never set foot on what had once been ours. I never dug for the treasure I buried as a boy-pirate. Never looked for the eagle that decorated the peak of the garage or the flag flying beneath. Never planted another bush or tree or carved a set of initials for *always*.

But memory requires no illegal trespassing, knows no boundaries. Like a night visitor memory returns to sift the past for clues. I feel certain that mother is a visitor there too. Where else on earth would she choose as a place of sweet return? Where else except the place where the memories of a lifetime were made? And sometime, I am sure, there will be a meeting of memory and spirit—perhaps beneath a certain dogwood tree.

We who once shared the same heartbeat believe it to be so.

Part One

The Early Years

The End of Something

BEFORE 1939 I thought of our driveway as my mother's domain for, up to that time, it had served only as a gravel path separating flower gardens. Then there were no ugly oil spots, no grease drippings; no heaving or buckling macadam. Just a length of flowers segregated according to sun, shadow and an ardent gardener's caprice. Even the sounds of the driveway were gentle sounds—the crunch of footsteps, bikes, scooters and wagons. The sound of birds too in the arch of over-hanging limbs. Wind chimes belling the day. The sound of people-talk and laughter.

The garage at the end of the drive was little more than a spacious tool shed for garden supplies and lesser machines. It stored folding lawn chairs, lawn mowers, sprinklers, bird baths and burlap bags. Summer things mostly. In winter the driveway was not shoveled up to the garage except where it met paths like the one leading to the burner out back or the places where deliveries were made—where the oil was piped into a tank in the cellar and the path that the neighbors used.

Up to 1939 our driveway was a feminine place; a beautiful place; a natural place; a living place.

But, in 1939 a car came into our lives, the very first we owned, a '39 Ford V-8, bright blue and wearing its New York World's Fair 1939 license plates in yellow and black. And, after that, our driveway became a macho place, a black-topped slab for squealing tires and grinding gears. Things were removed from the garage to make room for the car and before long a basketball hoop decorated the front of the garage, just above the doors. The blacktop soon became stained with oil and grease and there were residues of white foam from frequent car washings and waxings.

I, of course, was delighted with my father's belated burst of insight and wondered what took him so long to recognize the obvious—that automobiles were the best way to get around. Almost a necessity. And, more importantly, for a 16-year-old, a car was a symbol of prestige, an important part of the rites of passage. A car attracted the opposite sex. It won the respect of peers and elders. It radically altered the dimensions of time and space. A car was freedom on wheels. And, to top it all, gasoline was only ten cents per gallon in 1939.

But, even with a car in the driveway, my mother's claim to life and beauty was still honored. The crocuses continued to break through the crusted snow beside the house. Yellow trumpets of daffodils played the silent music of spring. Tulips, those perennials from ten or twelve past Mother's Days or Easters, unfolded once again to the morning sun. Other resurrections followed: jonquils, hyacinths, tiger lilies, daisies, black-eyed susans, mums, roses, yellow and red, sunflowers, wild, pink azaleas. And, overlooking it all, a dogwood and lilac bushes sweetening the air. Even the weeds had their place along the driveway. Some were useful—dandelion greens for salads; milkweed leaves for the silver chrysalis of the monarch butterfly.

Looking back almost sixty years I can see a symbolism that no one could possibly have seen then. For in a little over a month from the time we got our new car the world began to fall apart, the center no longer holding. Nazi Germany invaded Poland; Britain and France declared war on Germany and President Roosevelt proclaimed U.S. neutrality. The world was on its way toward a hell of its own making. There was a new and terrible word that the frightened world learned—*blitzkrieg*, the lightning war; the machine war.

But in America, we still had a few good years left and life went on much as it had. The Great Depression was slowly giving way to a wartime economy. We didn't know how

much was ending in 1939, that indeed, for millions, it was the
beginning of the end. We didn't realize that a world's innocence would be lost, never to be regained, not in all human
history. We didn't know that evil would eclipse the sun. We
didn't know that machines would crush the flowers. . .

In 1939 life expectancy was 59.7 years; the jet engine aircraft and the helicopter were invented; the best picture was
Gone With The Wind and the best songs, "Over the Rainbow"
and "God Bless America." The New York Yankees won the
World Series. The War was still an ocean away.

The machine had come to our driveway and all of us were
glad—all except our mother. She had a fear of machines. She
preferred things that had a heart. Friends had been killed in
automobile accidents. Her favorite grandmother had been
killed by a train. She was fascinated by the idea of flying, but
airplanes frightened her. She could not know at the time that
before long her only son would be a member of the Army Air
Forces.

Years later, after my father's stroke, he would ask: "Am I
going to spend the rest of my life in this driveway?" For he
was once an athlete and a traveler with no boundaries to his
life. But now there was no car in the driveway or in the
garage, just a lawn chair and a walker beside it—and the
answer to my father's anguished question was *yes*, his world
was reduced to the size of the driveway. And my mother was
his caregiver then and the machine was gone, but the flowers
were still there. His tears were my mother's tears as well: she
felt his pain as her own. But she did not miss the series of
shining machines that came after the '39 Ford. Her garden
was a garden again.

Then, after my father's death, there were no more automobiles except those of visitors. In the good weather my
mother lived outside in the driveway, tending her flowers
and probably dreaming of the time when the blossoms com-

peted with the machine. Thinking back perhaps to the passing of two World Wars and all the damage that machines had done to the flowers. Thinking too of the endurance of the flowers; how they survived the assaults of time and machine. Seeing how flowers had finally grown through the guns and tanks of Normandy. And the bones of the dead as well. Seeing that the weeds and flowers had taken over her driveway, sprouting through the cracks in the macadam. A fighting resurrection! A triumph of life over the machine. The day of the crocus delivered from pistons and gears.

And then my mother became a semi-invalid, confined to the driveway in the good weather. She and I spent hours, some of the best of our lives, talking and listening and remembering. And watching the flowers grow. I usually parked my car at the far end of the drive, near the street. It was out of sight there and did not offend the beauty of the place; did not spew its exhaust on people or flowers. My mother would tell me how, at night, she would listen for the sound of my bike and later, the car, coming home from some place or other. She would listen to the harmonies of homecoming and then go back to sleep, free at last from worry for another night. She had formed a separate peace with the driveway it seemed, and even looked forward to the gathering of kids in the driveway—warning them sometimes of trampling the flowers.

My mother faced eternity in the narrow strip of her driveway. There it was she spoke to God, family and friends. She remembered the best and worst of times there among the flowers and later, the tomato plants. She made her peace with past, present and future. And then she left us in her 100th year.

At my request the hearse pulled into the driveway on the way to the cemetery. A silent tribute to a great lady. It waited there for a minute or so before it backed out and continued on its way.

Now, the house is sold and strange things are happening at number 16. Most of the birch trees in the front yard have been taken down. The over-hanging branches have been pruned. Vinyl siding has been put on the two sides of the house my mother had never completed. Orange-colored stakes now mark the property line. There is a car in the garage and two vans in the driveway. And the driveway has been re-paved so that nothing grows between the cracks anymore, no struggling life. The white picket fence has been repaired and painted. The weeds have been uprooted. The bird feeders have been removed from the clothes line. But on either side of the driveway the flowers are still there! Like memory's blossoms they linger beside the blacktop stream that divides them.

But there are connections, even between strangers. There is a continuity of sorts, even between lives joined by a common driveway and a common house minus the memories.

Now when I come to town after the long winter's snows I drive by slowly. Perhaps I park around the corner and walk past. My mother's flowers come up each spring—crocuses, daffodils, tulips, hyacinths and the others. It is a ritual I would not miss. They return in all their splendor, *her* splendor. And, what is more, the strangers have fenced off the garden areas on either side of the drive and there are reflectors warning machine operators that life and beauty lie but inches away. And that glorious burst of color and the knowledge of a stranger who shares and cares is enough to inspire in me an Easter of the heart. Over the years I have learned that in endings there are also beginnings.

I just thought she would like to know.

A Rage of Roses

A ROSE isn't always a rose is a rose is a rose . . . Even the most delicate rose may give off its own special perfumes and visual beauty yet it has its thorns. And in this paradox there is a story, remembered and lived over and over again in my boyhood memories . . .

I must have been seven or eight years old when it happened. It was meant to be a surprise for my mother on Mothers' Day, the planting of a rosebush in the backyard. A living memorial of her favorite flower, a bleeding of beauty just outside her door.

I had saved my money earned by doing odd jobs, bought the rosebush and hid it in the garage, waiting for the big day. We didn't have a car in those Depression days so the garage, along with the attic, was a place to store things, surprises and memories, junk and treasure in curious juxtaposition.

In the morning I had told my next door neighbor and best friend, Dick, that I had bought a rosebush for my mother and that I planned to plant it, water it and put a fence around it, all while my mother was shopping.

My friend's face fell at the news. "I didn't know it was Mothers' Day," he said. And, turning his pockets inside out: "I don't have any money."

"Then make her something," I suggested. "Mothers like things you make."

"Like what?" he asked. "What can I make?"

I thought for a moment. "How about a napkin holder? Or something made for notes made out of clothespins? Paint her a picture. Make up a Mothers' Day story. Your mother'll be working all day so you'll have time."

A shadow of anxiety crossed his face. "She'll see your rose-bush out the window every day and she'll only get a drawing or a story." The injustice seemed evident the way he said it.

"She'll know you remembered," I told him. "That's the important thing."

He thought that over. "It's not the same," he said finally. And, despite his forced smile I got the feeling he was blaming me for something.

When Dick went away, presumably to create some gift for his mother, I planted my own surprise and put a fence of stakes around it. Then I watered it and finally stepped back to admire it, secretly thanking my dad for giving me the idea of a living bloom for a living mother. Then I went inside and waited for my mother's return.

She was late and I was anxious—eager to give her the present I had been hiding for the past three days. After a wait of ten minutes or so I decided to check on the view from the dining room, her rainy day perspective on my gift. But when I looked out the window there was nothing! No fencing; no roses; only a mysterious and revealing absence!

It took a moment or two for me to realize that the rosebush had been uprooted, cut to pieces and strewn over the lawn. And in a single moment the scene was a field of broken dreams. My heart fell. Then I saw him: Dick, in his own yard, throwing a ball against his garage and trying to catch it. And then I lost it—for the first time in my young life! I lost it completely!

A rage I had never known rose in me like a sudden tide, sweeping away everything but itself. Reason, sympathy, understanding—all were carried away in the furious undertow of the moment. I felt only my runaway heart; felt the scalding, angry tears blind my eyes. I felt fear too, the fear of losing control, of existing outside myself, beyond my emotional depths. The fear of being possessed by devils not my own!

I bolted out of the house, down the steps and across the yard. As I drew near him, Dick looked up at me and I could see his face was stained with tears, contorted by all he felt inside. I knew in that moment there would be no denials: he stood there in stoic anticipation, the classic victim, the martyr waiting for the final blow to fall.

Thank God I had no weapon in my hands, hands that now closed into fists and began swinging wildly. My legs were kicking too and strange sounds, primeval sounds were being torn from me in some language I had never known. The sounds were telling me to kill!

Then arms grabbed me from behind and I heard my mother's voice.

The spell was broken! The terrible enchantment suddenly gone! I was a child again, a child crying for himself and perhaps for another as well!

Dick ran off like a wounded animal. I collapsed on the lawn. My mother picked me up and carried me home.

It took an hour for her to calm me. I was calling Dick the ". . . enemy of my heart" and other names. But even as my anger was heaped on him and his deed, the fear was for myself and all that I had lost in that wild encounter, the explosion of anger that had ripped through me. And every time she tried to comfort me, the sobs started again. Then I would tell her once more about the planning, the preparation and the promise of the rosebush, now all gone!

"How about a tree?" The words came through my anger, doubt and confusion like the echoes of silence after a storm. Slowly I stopped sobbing with a sound like a motor stalling and I found myself listening to her words of healing.

"A maple tree."

"A tree?" I asked dumbly.

"We'll dig one up from behind the garage. A foot or so high. We'll plant it out front for all to see and admire."

I started to cry again. "No, the enemy of my heart will just dig it up again and then I'll have to—."

"No," she interrupted, "no he won't. His heart is broken too, dear. His heart will have to mend like yours. You'll have to be free and whole again, the both of you."

"He's the one who did it!" The words burst through the fury of remembrance. And it was then that I told her how Dick had forgotten it was Mothers' Day and how his mother was at work and he didn't know what to make for her and how the rosebush I was going to plant would always be a reminder of what he failed to do for her. And then I stopped, wondering if I was defending my enemy. "But I'll always hate him," I blurted out.

"Let's plant the tree," she said. "And then one day you and Dick will stand in its shade and look back and understand."

It was still Mothers' Day, I thought, and I had no present. And suddenly I wished that my father was there: he might not have been so quick to forgive and forget. Men were tougher that way and sometimes there was the need to stick together. Evil had to be punished before being forgiven. Otherwise there was no justice.

My mother tugged on my hand. "The tree," she said.

Together we planted the tree and over the years it grew straight and tall. But I wasn't there for the important parts of the story. A year or so later we moved away, not out of town but across town to a different neighborhood. Dick and I—we were never best friends again. Our paths didn't cross much after that although we attended the same high school. We moved in different circles. And when we did meet and talked about old times there was no mention of the War of the Roses. Not once! It was almost as though it never happened, yet it was there all the same, like an outcropping of estrangement, something between us. I didn't say anything about it and neither did he, and so, nourished by our benign neglect, the distance still grew.

And then there was college, a World War, the raising of families and the things we called "our lives."

I returned from time to time to visit my mother after my father's death. And, when I did, I went back to the old place to visit the tree we had planted. It was a beautiful green fountain of a tree now, that tree of the knowledge of good and evil, and I would touch its rough bark and a mantra of memories and prayers would spin through my head.

Dick and his family had moved away while I was in service and my mother had written that both his parents had died. His old home had a more prosperous look now—a deck out back and a screened-in porch. A pastel siding. Yet it looked poorer too, dwarfed by time and absence.

Dick and I—we met again. It was at our high school reunion. And even in all the din and confusion of greetings, Dick and I spent an hour or so together getting caught up on one another's lives. The meeting was cordial: we might have seemed best friends once more. As our conversation drew to a close, he asked me: "Have you been back?"

"Not yet," I said. "I've been helping Mom and seeing people. But I plan to make my pilgrimage before I leave."

After a farewell breakfast the next morning we got ready to leave. I felt the nagging pain of something left undone, something incomplete, something unsaid. We had talked *around* what was really on our minds but we hadn't talked *about* it. And so it was still there.

We shook hands and then hugged—suddenly and unexpectedly coming together like two magnets inching toward their critical distance.

The next day I visited the tree. I pulled to the side of the road, crossed the sidewalk and approached the living memory. I circled around the tree to view it from the other side, the house side. I was surprised to see a smooth place where the bark had been cut away, a background for two sets of initials made with small nails driven into the trunk—Dick's and mine!

I looked at it for minutes, almost in disbelief, then ran my hand over the nails like a blind man reading braille. Suddenly I heard a cough and startled, turned around.

There was a friendly face. "It's O.K.," he said. "I live here. I gave him permission to do it. He said you used to live here too. He said that this was like a memorial tree."

"Thanks," I nodded. And, as I turned to go I noticed a few golden scabs of maple sap still oozing from the nail holes like a stigmata from an ancient wound, now healed.

Ante-Bellum

A *nte-bellum:* before the war, usually the Civil war.

One of my fondest memories is that of a "date" I once had with my mother to see the now-classic film *Gone With the Wind*. It was opening night, a gala affair, at the Palace Theatre in Albany, New York, and I remember wearing a suit and tie especially for the occasion and I remember my mother all dressed up too, even to the corsage I pinned on her earlier. That was way back in 1939—just before the world went mad.

Those were the *ante-bellum* days too.

There were the usual local celebrities at the Palace that evening—political and business leaders in the community; a few New York City actors and a well-known film critic. Doctors and lawyers; enough of the establishment to impress a high school student and his mother. Some wore formal clothing and drove up in long, black cars or taxis. There were spotlights rigged up to catch the celebrities in cones of light and there were people being interviewed by local radio announcers. For many reasons it was an evening to be remembered. . .

Over the years that evening *did* turn into a cherished memory, aged and sweetened by time. My mother and I were young and together; the film was grand and impressive, one of the first I had ever seen with its high drama enhanced by color and an half-hour intermission during which people milled around and discussed an ancient war and what had gone before. It was a kind of fantasy evening, with all the glitz and glamour usually reserved for Hollywood or New York City openings. And I remember wondering how the premiere played in Atlanta and whether the burning of that city and Sherman's march to the sea rekindled for some the angry fires of memory.

Most people had read the book before the movie was released: it was a huge bestseller and no book, then or now, was talked about more. Certainly almost everyone had heard of it, that romantic and dramatic account of the end of the Old South, a civilization "gone with the wind." Because of the popularity of the novel, expectations ran high. My mother and I didn't realize it at the time but our world too, the *ante-bellum* world of 1939 was about to be taken on the wind—or perhaps, more accurately, on the *whirlwind*.

Memory is highly selective, of course, and account of that must be taken. And memory is also enduring. Not long ago I was attending an Air Force Reunion in Macon, Georgia and I was impressed by the treasury of memories and images that still survived from those *ante-bellum* days: the belief in traditional Southern hospitality and charm; the lovely *ante-bellum* mansions with all of their history intact; the public statues and pictures of Robert E. Lee and other heroes of the Confederacy. The stories that have refused to die and have even taken on a life of their own. The public holidays that many still honor. And all the private and obscure shrines that memory creates and holds on to. All in celebration of a time, a place and a way of life now gone with the wind.

And now, almost sixty years after that film opening in a Northern city I find myself remembering and making emotional and even historical connections with the past and in what was lost or gained. But things are different now: my mother is gone, and there is still an enormous absence in my life. But memories are like jewels, to be taken out and examined or even polished and worn once in a while . . .

1939. Despite the gathering storm and the atrocities that were a prelude to the Nazi invasion of Poland on September 1 there was a spirit of remarkable innocence, even naivete, in

America in those days. We were emerging from the Great Depression and we were separated from warring factions by two oceans. We had stuck our heads in the sand and were hoping that all the problems and conflicts would disappear. Only the more perceptive among us read the signs correctly and their voices were usually stilled by the crowds who did not or would not hear the bell tolling for us as well.

Before the war; before Pearl Harbor. Before the Holocaust; before the Bomb. Before the assigned guilt at the Nuremberg war trials—. Innocence, like Paradise, cannot usually be regained. The people have changed and the world has changed and there is no going back. You can't un-ring a bell. We did not know it—a boy and his mother at the movies—but the picture we were seeing was prophetic. Like the *ante-bellum* South ours too would be a world gone with the wind.

Another writer, Charles Dickens, had written that the time of one of his fictions was the best of times, the worst of times. And so it was in 1939. It was "the best of times; it was the worst of times." Looking back on it all, it was a time of injustice; poverty; racism and other crimes against the human spirit. But it was a time too when we believed we were responsible for our actions and in control of our destinies. A time when we, with God's help, had a chance of solving our problems. A time before events seemed to grow to control, even dominate our lives. And it was a time when most of us turned to someone or something greater than ourselves—from love or fear or even the agony of doubt.

I have heard many of my own generation saying it: **"It's a different world!"** And then they would go on to say that, even with all the cruelty and misery and loss of the greatest war in human history there was still pain humanized, joy humanized. There was a feeling of being in it together, of shared suffering. There was a sense of community that we have not known since. It was almost as though, on a person-

al level, those hard and terrible times brought about a soft-
ening of the heart, a sympathy, an empathy. . .

Like all young men or women I was reluctant to admit
that a way of life could be swept away by the wind. Or a love
like that of Scarlet and Rhett could be over. So that it was all
finally and irrevocably gone. I preferred to think that what
was blown away would be blown back, that the wind was a
vagrant wind, now from the east, now from the west—and
finally balancing out like an equation. For young people do
not usually think in terms of permanence: for them the
happy ending is just over the rainbow. The young do not
look back over the ruins with the historian's critical eye: they
see time and the human experience called "life" as ebb and
flow, the happier tides of youth. And I remember telling my
mother as we left the theater that Scarlet and Rhett would
probably get back together again, perhaps at Tara, and in
some brighter tomorrow.

"Perhaps," she told me, a little solemnly, I thought. "It's
good to think so."

And there was a great tolerance and kindness in that
maternal neutrality of hers. In some way she seemed to know
that a painful awareness took both time and tears.

There may be a danger of reading in too much, of giving
too great a significance to what was a simple event held in
memory. There may be a tendency to read in deep allegories
and symbols, to see ghosts in the darker corners. Just as there
is a tendency to see one's life as symbolic of all human life
and experience. Yet that is what we must do sometimes: we
must proceed from the particular to the general. For the person who speaks or writes about his/her own life and times is
really the only one who truly speaks or writes of everyone
and *all* times. I have held on to this particular *ante-bellum*
memory because it involves a world I once knew and a relationship between a mother and son, a relationship that

shaped me into what I became and what I still am. And that is the best of reasons for not only remembering but also for celebrating the past. And learning from it as well.

Ante-bellum, before the war. In the lives of those who have experienced war and its aftermath it is a Latin phrase that sings like a benediction, a blessing. It describes an idyllic time, a time forever remembered and sometimes defined by our fervent desire for peace on earth and happiness. For some it is the very measure of time remembered—*before, during* and *after* the war, almost rivaling the traditional B.C. and A.D. of our Christian heritage. The words seem to ring like bells on a solemn holiday—Christmas perhaps, or Easter. *Ante-bellum.* There is even the sound of prayer in it.

But even in solemnity there is the faint, languished call to remembrance; a call to those quieter sounds and softer images that rise to the surface of our lives. For, just as in the hell of battle a soldier may notice a butterfly lit on his rifle barrel or be drawn to the way the sun shines on an approaching sandy shore, so a person may return on the wings of remembrance to a time of make-believe or a time of special closeness to another. An *ante-bellum* time perhaps when a mother and a son shared a war story—a story that was and a story yet to come—and made a lasting memory one evening before the darkness fell.

The Shrinking Christmas Tree

IF my memory serves me, our family started out with a real, six-foot Christmas tree and ended up with an artificial tree of no more than six inches. It didn't happen over night: the shrinkage took half a century and the influence of two generations of spiritual women who never gave up.

I still remember that Christmas tree of my childhood—the beautiful, delicate ornaments; the red, white and green lights; the dripping, silvery, tinsel icicles; the artificial snow—all topped with a star of wonder. There were a few Santas perched on balsam branches, a few snowmen, a few reindeer, a few ballet dancers, a few wooden soldiers, a few strings of popcorn and cranberries and some paper rings. It was, for the most part, a secular tree, a children's tree. It echoed the society's materialistic concerns, its standards of worth and ways of celebration. It was an image reflected in the mirror of the outside world, the image presented in the slick magazines, popular imaginations and, later, television. It was, for those who could afford it in those hard times, an American ideal, an American way of celebrating Christmas.

Yet someone had surreptitiously hung a small, cardboard Nativity scene from a bent paper clip on an inconspicuous branch near the back of the tree, a reminder, barely noticeable under a single star. Someone had dropped a hint, a clue that there might be something more than glitz, glitter and presents under the tree, a kind of silent contradiction to the tree as it appeared. If not a contradiction, then a shift in focus, a reminder that things were not always as they appeared. It was a protest also, albeit a quiet one, like the Biblical voice crying in the wilderness or the high and dignified lyricism of the loyalist, Ruth, clinging to her mother-in-law's people and their beliefs: ". . . whither thou goest, I will go . . . thy people shall be my people and thy God my God . . ."

I suspected Mama, my maternal grandmother until she was no longer with us, and then my suspicion fell on my mother. Certainly it wasn't my sister or I for we were the beneficiaries of the newer attitudes, the newer celebrations. We did not question what showered down on us. We were happy in our plenty. We initiated no hints of change.

As the years passed, I noticed the Christmas tree kept getting smaller and the Nativity scene kept getting larger in what seemed to be an inverse ratio. I noticed also that the number of store-bought gifts was smaller as the home-made gifts became more in number—the samplers; the photographs; the original stories; the baked goods; the spiritual bouquets; the charitable donations in someone's name. I noticed that the cemeteries where our dead rested received more flowers, more visitations. Gradually, as the tree became smaller, the creche became an object of attention and special interest. Its very smallness called attention to itself—as a small person might call attention to himself in a land of giants. The Nativity scene did not shine or glitter. It did not blink in color. It was just there, surrounded by a mixed crowd of believers, shepherds and kings. A whisper in a tumult, an echo from 2000 years ago. A reminder of other voices, other times.

Something else happened too: the Nativity scene broke away from the tree and began to re-assemble itself under an eastern star. First there was a simple, wooden frame. Then a straw-filled manger that held an infant watched over by his parents and those gathered, celebrants of the miraculous birth—the miniature, alabaster figures of animals, shepherds, kings and the Magi. Piece by piece it grew until it seemed to challenge the tree itself and, as the secular influence of the tree seemed to diminish, the spiritual influence of the family veneration seemed to rise like a swelling hymn. The star appeared brighter; the shepherds and animals more numer-

ous and appropriate; the Magi more resplendent in their
exotic robes; the Holy Family more a projection of those we
knew or imagined. As the secular influences seemed to
diminish, the spiritual influences became more prominent.
And so it continued over the years . . .

By now our children had children of their own and there
was a long parade of leaving to balance the new life coming—grandparents, a father, an aunt died young and our
beloved Mama. And as mother moved into her eighties and
then into her nineties the tree grew smaller and smaller while
the creche was expanding into a crowd of figures that
seemed to overflow the barn. With Mama gone, suspicion
had fallen on mother as the one responsible for the elevation
of the Nativity scene. All of her influence seemed directed
toward the preservation of religious holidays as sacred. She
would not exile Santa Claus but she would reduce him to a
fat, jolly folk hero. She would not banish the Easter bunny
but she would relegate it to the land of joyful make-believe.
She would not scare away the ghosts and goblins of
Halloween but she would remember the dead with love and
not fright. She would not make a candy-fest of St. Valentine's
Day. She was perfectly willing to give to the world the things
that were the worlds as long as we also rendered to God the
things that were God's. And she tried her best to have her
family see the spiritual forest for the single trees.

In some ways her mission was apocalyptic, a revelation to
her children, for we too began to see beneath the surface of
things and sound depths we had not known. We were
encouraged to see the extraordinary in the ordinary; to see
the exalted in the humble; the profound in the simple; the
spiritual in the material.

But that was then and this is now.

For the years since mother's leaving we have celebrated
our family Christmas at our older daughter's house, where a

minor miracle happened in the form of a new, yet old orna-
ment on the beautiful and full Christmas tree. It was an old
scrap of yellow paper bearing the greeting "MERRY
CHRISTMAS" in mother's hand. It was a scrap of paper
found in one of her boxes of "things" randomly willed to all
of us. It was also a message across the great gulf of space and
time. Her greeting from the other side reminded us that the
last words too might be delivered in tongues and that each of
us was free to translate as we chose.

Now the tree is huge and beautifully decorated with ornaments from different generations of different families joined
by love. But the creche is there too in all its rustic glory and
there is no tension between them. And, although Ruth has
closed her book of life there are now others—Hannah and
her little brother Jacob to ponder the mystery of the plain and
simple greeting hung from a prominent branch of such an
elegant tree.

My Mother's Mother

I BEGIN with a grandmother's tale, a tale she used to tell me a long time ago, one she called "The Juggler of Notre Dame." It is the story of a homeless man, a simple man of faith and a street juggler who performed to an indifferent audience on the crowded streets of Paris for a scattering of coins, barely enough to keep him alive.

On a day set aside to honor the Virgin Mary one of the priests at Notre Dame Cathedral discovered this ragged man juggling balls and rings before the statue of Our Lady. The astonished priest reprimanded the juggler, saying that this holy place was not a place to profane by practicing an art reserved for theatres and the streets.

"I am sorry, Father," the juggler replied sadly, "but I have nothing else to offer Our Lady, on this Her day, but the talent I live by, a talent that the Lord, in His mercy, has graciously given me."

The priest thought for a moment and then was surprised to find himself apologizing to the juggler for his own hasty words. "I am sorry too," he said. "Sorry for speaking without thinking. You are right, my friend. Our Lady accepts any gift that comes from the heart, as I am sure yours does. Please—" He made a gesture that gave the juggler his tacit permission to continue and then left him to his unique offering.

And then my grandmother would come up with one of her supporting quotations that seemed to be preserved in her memory like bronzed echoes. "So you see, it is not what we do that makes us holy. We make holy what we do." She did not use the word *consecration* at the time. I would not have known what she meant. But that was what she was talking about—setting apart as sacred; to hallow; to devote or dedicate. We make holy what we do if we do the right thing for the right reason. The juggler in her story had consecrated his talent by offering it on the altar at Notre Dame. His performance had been sacrificial and by offering it he had elevated a humble street art into an act worthy of grace.

Her quotation was meant to expand and enrich her story like a stone dropped in a pond, a stone making ever-widening circles that finally reach the shore. Many years later I learned that my grandmother's quote was taken from Meister Eckhart, a theologian whose lessons were often contained in a nugget of wisdom. And I feel certain she knew that the reaction to both her story and her quotation would be a delayed one, perhaps for decades or for as long as it took for a boy to grow to manhood. But she was a patient woman, a patient storyteller and was always willing to wait even for decades for her words to take effect.

There was a message implicit in her story as well: just as the juggler had consecrated his art by making it an act of devotion so I should strive to do the right thing—and for the right reason as well. My grandmother had given me a rare insight into my own ability to dedicate the simplest act into one sacrificial and profound. She was telling me that I had this special power I never knew I had—and I might obtain the glory and grace that went with it as well. It was an awareness that changed my life and, at times, weighed heavily on me and confused me. I could make holy what I did by an act of dedication: it was a powerful effect in the heart and soul of a boy.

But what talent did I have? I was just a boy with a talent for boyish things like idleness, play, reading and daydreaming. What if I had no special talent? What if I was just an ordinary person? That was what I wondered then. I know better now. The experience of living has taught me that "ordinary" people are indeed the "salt of the earth," "the light of the world." A Lord's chosen. Were not the Lord's disciples recruited from these ranks, mostly fishermen who became fishers of men. Not a prince among them. And I know enough of both war and peace to know that heroes also come from the ranks of the "ordinary." There were decorated soldiers who, only months before had been mail carriers, clerks, teachers, students, merchants and candy makers. There were saints, now eligible for veneration, canonized and capable of interceding for people on earth, who had been sinners. There were martyrs who paraded the stained-glass windows of cathedrals who had once been among those who denied or betrayed a risen Lord. There is no gene for heroism, sainthood or martyrdom. *We make holy what we do.*

Many special talents remain hidden until there is a crisis and only then do they rise to the surface suddenly and without a conscious summoning, a response to the moment's urgent need. Sometimes there are hints of a latent talent—a singing voice; a sense of holiness; a rare imagination; an unusual sense of balance; an athletic ability. But there needs to be an opportunity for those talents to be recognized and used.

And there are the quiet, the healing talents that often go unnoticed yet mean so much in our frequently indifferent world. A talent for listening. A talent for sympathetic understanding; for waiting with the anxious; for speaking with the lonely. And sometimes the enormous talent of just being there for another, a physical presence to fill the void. A hand to hold. There are the caregivers as well, those who care for others by giving of themselves. And, as a great poet pointed out, ". . . they also serve who only stand and wait."

There are those whose lives are spent performing low-status menial tasks that no one else wants, all those who sweep, shovel and clean up after the rest of us. Everything may be an offering if we dedicate it in the right spirit, even our humble tasks, our prayers and yes, even our suffering when all else is gone. *We make holy what we do.*

In a sense we are all jugglers, for it is a talent that is needed in this life, perhaps a talent demanded by life itself. Not necessarily the talent for juggling balls, rings or plates but the talent or art for keeping two or more things in the air at one time. We all do it. The philosopher is a juggler; so is the theologian. And many of us juggle good and evil, right and wrong, God and mammon. Duty and desire. The real art is to juggle as honestly as possible and with a minimum of illusion; to keep the trickery and self-deception out of our lives and our art. And to dedicate our talent and its effects to something beyond ourselves, an offering to others.

Years after my grandmother's story, years after her leaving, and after some false starts I became a juggler of ideas and words. Years later I was to write a poem in memory of my early companion and saintly storyteller. It was based on the story she told me—and it was based too on what she was, herself—a woman of love, faith and art. Called simply "Juggler," it went like this:

"Whatever goes up must come down:
Equally true of memories, promises, colored balls, clubs
    and rings.
The children laugh their wonder;
Others smile, certain they understand
As the juggler's burning eyes trace
The sanctity of motion and balance, remembering
That once a Lady smiled Her Grace
In answer to his faith and art."

Ceremonial Trees

NOT long after my mother's death I planted a maple seedling in her back yard as a memorial, knowing full well her house would be sold within the year. Perhaps my offering was from guilt as much as anything, guilt because I could not live there myself and had to surrender it to strangers. Perhaps it was from the absence that followed her leaving. Perhaps for the sake of what I considered my newly established rite. But this way the tree would remain, a surrogate heir to stand guard over what for sixty years had been her home. In the eight years that have passed I have never returned, but that tree has grown in memory, for memory is where the past lives.

Dad liked trees well enough, but in what he thought was their proper setting, namely a forest, woods or manicured yard. He didn't care much for nature in the raw. But, all to his credit, he didn't care if others did. And he wasn't all that concerned with memorials: he believed a person built his own during a lifetime. And that was what he tried to do.

My mother had always loved trees, especially maples. "They bleed so sweetly; they turn so beautifully," she told me once in a memorable phrase. I didn't know what she meant until I tasted maple syrup or watched the fires of autumn consume what had been a summer's growth.

As a child I thought that the tree planting tradition was original with me for I began to observe it when I was very young, too young to know much about the Great Depression, that time of want and wishes. I knew only that there weren't many ways for a boy to earn money for presents on Christmas, birthdays, Mothers' Day, Fathers' Day and all those other days when a gift was required. There were homemade cards, of course, made with shirt cardboards and crayons, cards that might be tucked away in family bibles, drawers, journals and memory. But I favored *living* things—plants, flowers and the greatest of all growing things, trees. And, best of all they were free except for the labor of getting them, the anxiety of nursing them through the critical time to see if they would end up as stick or tree. And I thought there was something spiritual about trees, even before I committed to memory those lines of Joyce Kilmer's that tell how the tree ". . . looks at God all day, and lifts its leafy arms to pray . . ."

My first memorial tree I planted when I was in third grade, when Kathy, a classmate, died of some sudden and mysterious childhood disease. I considered her my "girlfriend" and I was bewildered and devastated by her loss. Having no previous experience with death I figured that life might be its antidote and therefore the best of all gifts. I went to the woods and selected a small birch that was intertwined with another: to me it seemed like nature's own sculpture of arboreal first love. I planted it one summer's night when her family was at their camp, but when I went back a few days later it was gone! It remains one of my sorrowful mysteries and I lived with the pain of it until I was old enough to understand that not all mysteries were for solving.

My second memorial tree was for Mama, one of my spiritual mentors whom I loved and to whom I was very close as a boy. My mother had gone to Los Angeles all the way from Albany, New York alone and by train to bring her mother home to die. I had a job then and had started a family of my own so I couldn't accompany her, much as I wanted to. But my prayers and my imagination went with her, along every mile of railroad track. And when Mama died I went to a mountain overlook called Indian Ladder and consecrated with a prayer a tall, stately evergreen that bent to the prevailing west winds and I carved her name and then highlighted my work with nails that reflected the setting sun.

My third memorial tree was called *CaN wakaN kiN*, in Lakota, the Holy Tree. I planted it in the dry, flinty soil of a South Dakota Indian Reservation. It was a cottonwood and I planted it along the banks of the Little White River that winds through a canyon surrounded by buttes and sky. My deceased friend's first choice would have been a tree burial like the ones in the days when the People decided those things for themselves. He didn't like the idea of being buried beneath the ground, afraid that his spirit would be "buried with his bones" and would not be able to find its way over the Spirit Trail. So I did what I thought was the next best thing to a tree burial: I wrote his name and a few words in his language, put it into a buffalo hide pouch that his grandfather had given him, tied it with a leather thong to the cottonwood. Then I planted it near the river bank where it would always be watered. It was a quiet and peaceful place where the river sang a gurgling song as it went over the rocks and then, in winter, it froze into a deep, white silence. I thought my friend might appreciate the contrast.

Then there were trees I did not plant but gave to others as ceremonial trees. Together with other members of my class I helped in giving a tree and a plaque to my college. And, over the years I have contributed to a fund to protect the giant redwoods in California and the forests of my own Adirondack Mountains. My wife and I have given gifts of trees to my daughter who owns her own home—trees delivered, planted and guaranteed by an arborist or landscape contractor. The trees will offer beauty, privacy and shade over the years and hopefully will also cast memories with their shadows. But it's not the same somehow, not the same as going out in the woods with a pail and shovel and a heart full of anticipation. Not the same as digging your own, careful not to cut the roots. Not the same as nursing it along as you would an infant. Of seeing it climb with the seasons.

Once, for a gift, I bought one of those dwarfed trees for indoors, to be grown in a pot. I don't remember if it bore fruit or not. I bought it as a present for my mother but never gave it to her because of something she said as we passed an indoor tree in a shopping mall.

"It seems so lonely in the crowd, such a stranger to sky. You feel like going over to see if it's real."

A few days later I gave the dwarfed tree to a person who admired it once, calling it "cute."

In my daughter's garden there are perennials—flowers, shrubs, bushes—all taken from my mother's yard and transplanted. A kind of bouquet of continuing generations, colored in memories. Each spring they seem to glorify the life cycle by their budding. The next best thing to having her return.

I have never much liked cut flowers, never liked to send them or even receive them. For cut flowers are dying flowers, their brief lives prolonged by an envelope of powder and maybe a scent artificially induced. My mother did not like them either. She used to call them "death warmed over" and she much preferred a dirt covered tulip bulb that looked like a grenade, one that might explode into possibilities and border her driveway with color.

Mother's love for trees was with her all her long life, even to the last days. I would wheel her to the solarium, the sunroom where patients gathered to warm themselves in the winter sun and lifetime memories. Outside the huge picture window was a solitary tree, barren, leafless, a skeleton of its summer self. It seemed to shake and shiver in the cruel February wind. Mother would stare at that tree as though it were a fountain of leaves rising. She would stare until the sun died in the web of its branches. Only then would she be ready to have me wheel her back to her room. But, by then I too knew enough of ceremonial trees to recognize one enduring the last few pangs of winter for the requiem of a healing spring.

The Latin Teacher

BONDING between a parent and son can sometimes come about in predictable ways. In my case, as in many others, bonding with my father came about through our mutual interest and participation in athletics, especially tennis. In fact, at one point in our lives we were both tennis professionals and registered members of the United States Professional Lawn Tennis Association. But there were other sports: football, baseball, boxing, wrestling and basketball that drew us closer together. My dad was my first coach; my first personal trainer; my first teammate and my first real friend.

In contrast, in a way that couldn't be predicted at all, my mother and I arrived at our close relationship through deeper channels.

When I was a rebellious, aimless high school student looking for an easy way to meet the language requirement, I suddenly recalled that my mother had once been a Latin teacher as well as a classical scholar. How could I have forgotten? The evidence was everywhere—in the dusty books that lined the shelves. In the solemn Latin quotations and inscriptions in her books and taped to the refrigerator door and even in the cryptic notes she wrote to herself and that she alone could translate. In her speech, spiced with classical quotes and formal sounding declarations. And I thought that in some, as yet undetermined way, I might use all that latent learning to my advantage, to help make my own academic burdens lighter, leaving me more time for athletics and girls. So I began to ponder the possibilities of how she might help me with the mysteries of translations, conjugations, declensions, vocabulary and routine homework assignments. She might even help me compose oh-so-clever lines, lines fashioned after Ovid, about eternal love, perhaps to impress the pretty girls in my class. Reasons enough to bear the boredom of a language swept into the dustbin of history. So I signed up for Latin.

My friends warned me that the other choices, French and Spanish were easier and, as "living" languages might be more practical. But, for the first time in my life I chose the dead over the living, the far over the near. It was only much later that I discovered I had misjudged several critical factors—my mother's inordinate love for the written word and my own reluctance to take advantage of someone I loved.

I had at times wondered why it was that she was so attracted to a language spoken only by priests, petulant schoolboys, scholars and backward-looking college majors. And perhaps, I suspected, by those bookish, horn-rimmed librarians who shushed us from their stacks. And I wondered, too, how a grocer's daughter from a small town in Northern New York State came to love the culture and classics of Rome and Greece. By what destiny, accident or curious turn of events? Certainly she was kissed by no Mediterranean or Aegean breezes that inclined her that way. For she was no traveler except perhaps a time traveler. Was it the father who died so young I did not even remember him? Was he the one determined that his daughters, even with the dark clouds of World War I gathering, would be college graduates, the first in the family? Certainly no sunny climes seduced her from the long, harsh winters of Oswego where the snowfalls were measured in stories rather than feet. It had to come from somewhere—this ear for language, this sensitivity for words, these flights of the imagination. Her own Irish mother raised her daughters on the myths and tales of Ireland, along with the lives of the saints. But, no matter the impulse responsible for it, my mother looked to the classics for inspiration and beauty, and she looked to Latin and Greek as the vehicles of their deliverance.

But, to the Latin teacher's son Latin was only a kind of echo-talk down the corridors of time, useful, some claimed, because it helped one to understand the grammatical infra-structure of other languages. Yet I couldn't understand why it was that my mother, whose judgment I so respected, loved those same lonesome echoes? Sometimes I was forced to admit that those Latin words and phrases had a certain strength, dignity and even a stately beauty. But even beauty should have a function I had decided by the time I was six-teen.

I asked her about it one day, the reason she was so attract-ed to a language no infant would ever learn, no sculptor engrave—

"Like *'E pluribus unum?'* " she interrupted, smiling. Then she translated: "Out of many, one. Our motto."

"And forgotten names," I went on.

"Like Caesar, Virgil and Marcus Aurelius," she asked.

Realizing that I would never win the battle of relevance, I surrendered. And just in time. For my mother fired her big guns—fifteen or twenty lines from *The Aeneid,* for which I had no return fire.

But my scheme worked. My mother put down her cross-word puzzles, philosophy and detective stories and dusted off her Latin grammars, trots, dictionaries and church Latin. And I was the reluctant beneficiary of all that resurrected knowledge and for a time I staggered under its weight.

I needed only two years of a language to meet the require-ments. I ended up taking three. And for my big Latin project I wrote a story in Latin about a Roman soldier who witnessed Christ's crucifixion and became a convert to what would become Christianity. I wrote the story on my own mostly, with a few grammatical assists from mother. Caesar's ghost must have turned over in his tomb. My story was published in the literary section of the school paper and the dead language had risen to form a living bond between mother and son.

There were collateral effects of what had become our common interest in things classical. My mother and I attended performances of *Julius Caesar* and *Macbeth* at a local university. I began to write stories, even though most were about flying or sports. What had begun as a selfish strategy had exceeded itself: an interest in Latin had expanded to include "literature" and, even as a beginning storyteller I recognized a familiar theme—what begins as an attempt to deceive sometimes brings positive results. The young thief who had attempted to steal his mother's knowledge discovered that knowledge is worth pursuing for its own sake. And, in our common search, my mother re-discovered things as well. She had re-discovered the anguish and eventual joy of waiting for her soldier overseas. She re-discovered the reasons why the classics had been the foundation of her formal education. And she discovered the things in her son that lay beneath the surface.

As I approached the end of my secondary education, my mother suggested I take a series of aptitude tests and, although they were an additional expense during what were lean years, I took them seriously for her sake and did my best to give accurate answers. But, at the time, I could not take the results seriously for they pointed to a life of the mind rather than a life of action. A teacher, especially a college teacher: that was the first recommendation. Up to that time when I thought in terms of a "career," I thought of aviation or professional athletics. The results of the tests astonished me and I dismissed them; however I did not dismiss my mother's efforts and her sacrifice. A World War and an aborted business career later I would once again listen to those voices from the past, those reverberating echoes.

I did become a college professor and an author. My mother's intuition had proven as reliable as modern testing techniques. And sometimes, when I am tempted to take credit for those new directions in my life or assign them to other causes—accident, fate, luck or serendipity—I remember the Latin teacher who once shared a heartbeat, a home and a hearth. I remember her love and her faith in me. And I remember the times she read to me after my father and I had finished throwing the football or baseball in the back yard. I remember that she not only led me to church, but to God. She was my Greek Moirae. She was Clotho, the Spinner, who spun the thread of life. And I remember, too, that for a while we shared a dead language and formed a living, lasting connection.

When my mother left home for the last time it fell to me to peel the years of clippings from her refrigerator. One of the oldest, most brittle clippings was a quotation from Virgil's *Aeneid*. It translated: "They are able because they think they are able." A Virgilian truth from a Roman poet across the centuries and almost buried on a 20th century refrigerator that stored the food of life for both body and spirit.

A Sort of Autobiography

MY mother left behind a sort of autobiography in the form of notes, snippets and scraps of paper tucked away in drawers and between the pages of books, magazines and old calendars. These scraps were seldom addressed to a specific member of the family—which meant they were for *anyone* or *everyone*. It was almost as if mother were playing an elaborate game of who-am-I? For each note revealed a part of her personality or character. In some notes we were given a clue to some past event and it was our job to reconstruct that event, to remember and celebrate it with her again. The notes were hardly ever dated or signed: it was up to the finder to interpret the words written in her bold and recognizable hand.

". . . sometime I want to go to Wilkes-Barre again. When I'm an old, old lady I want to go."

This was written on the back of a ten-year old calendar page and alluded to an event in June of 1943 in the City of Wilkes-Barre, Pennsylvania. She wanted to return because it was the scene of one of her grandest and proudest moments in her close relationship with her son.

In May of 1943 I completed my basic training at Keesler Field in Biloxi, Mississippi and was sent north to begin my Air Cadet training at Bucknell Junior College in Wilkes-Barre. I had been gone for almost four months and my parents were delighted that I was coming to a place close enough for them to visit during a wartime period of strict rationing. They were also delighted that our unit would be quartered in the same hotel in which they would be staying, the Hotel Sterling, at the time, Wilkes-Barre's finest. So they spent their precious gasoline stamps and drove the five hours from their home in Upstate New York.

We had dinner together on Friday night and they met some of my friends I had written them about. They even met my commanding officer, a Captain John Smith. They watched me fly a Piper Cub at a nearby airport and they saw the Air Cadets parade on Saturday morning in a local park.

My father, a veteran of World War I swelled with pride as we marched past a reviewing stand and a large audience of applauding townspeople. We were singing the Army Air Corps song about the ". . . wild, blue yonder" and other places we didn't know much about at the time. My father related to me how inspiring, patriotic it all was, a glory moment, the sort he had once known. And my mother had been visibly moved: it proved to be a defining moment in our close relationship, one of our finest hours, a moment to be bronzed in memory. The whole weekend was, for her, a time of great joy and quiet pride in her son's new role as aviator and soldier, a time when anticipation and reality met, accompanied by marshal music, drama and pride to become the stuff of memories. For a few days in a strange city I was hers again, the son who had gone off one day into the stark and anonymous oblivion of war. She had never seen me in uniform, never met those comrades I had written about in letters, never witnessed the energy and enthusiasm of youth as they prepared for a war they could not imagine. She was as innocent as all of us: that and her love was the bond between us. My father, who had served overseas in France in the field artillery, seemed to be marching to the sound of a different drummer. And I noticed my mother, trying to read his solemn look, even with the music sounding "Over There," a song of World War I. But, for her, it was a magic moment and we were its heroes defending a way of life and the moment. The whole world was caught up in history's greatest conflict and she and one of her own were a part of it—as her husband had been a generation before. And, although I could usually read my mother's emotions I could only imagine all that she was feeling that weekend, the pride and the glory. And when we went to Mass on Sunday morning she lit a candle for me and, as she did, I could see on her face that she had come to terms with all the doubts and fears of what might be and that she had accepted whatever was to come. And that too was a moment for framing.

I did not return to Wilkes-Barre until our first reunion in 1993, fifty years after our "Fly Boys" as the townspeople had affectionately named us, had marched through their city. By then our ranks were decimated. Some never made it back from the war. Others had surrendered to the strict arrests of time and disease. My mother was then an old, old lady, already afflicted with the disease that would erase her memory and eventually take her life. For a moment or two I thought of escorting her back to Wilkes-Barre—but that was only a momentary triumph of hope over experience. Finally my better judgment prevailed: I decided against it.

Even though I was aware that you can't go home again, the people of Wilkes-Barre tried their best to make it a real homecoming. The newspapers, radio stations and television had publicized our return and those who remembered the war years welcomed us back. We marched, singing once more of comrades who "went down in flames" as the Air Corps song predicted they might. And the Hotel Sterling?

It was still there—part of it a residence for Seniors. The rest of it was closed. Old faces looked out windows where torn curtains seemed to be signaling a surrender to the winds of change and chance. The City, ravaged by a flood in the seventies, had not prospered in the years since we left. The downtown area where we marched through cheering crowds was run-down and many businesses were boarded up. People had moved to the suburbs and the inner City was in a sad state of decline. I was even told by one old timer that beneath the City's square the fires of old coal mines still burned. I do not know the truth of that, but I do know that old memories still burned somewhere beneath the surface.

When I got back home I made up stories for my mother, fiction to feed her imagination. Disillusion turned to illusion. After all, space and time are finally measured by the heart. I did not mention the old faces that peered from lonely windows. I did not mention the airmen missing. I did not mention the City's decline.

"Was there music? Bands playing?" she wanted to know.

"Yes," I told her, "And the sound of cadences counted and marching feet. Things hadn't changed that much."

I did not lie. The music was inside me.

There was still another written fragment I have committed to memory, another sentence in her piecemeal autobiography. Translated from the silence it said: "Yes, I do remember now that there was such a person as I." She wrote those words in September of 1995, the year before she died, the year she was suffering most and in the terrible grip of her dementia. And in that single, sad sentence there were two people—the "I" that remembers and the "I" remembered. In that sentence also was the tragedy of a little girl lost.

I always thought my mother would make a great writer but she chose to speak rather than write. Writing is a lonely occupation while speaking has a social context, an exchange between people, an affair of breath. Words seemed to travel from mind and heart to mouth, not from mind to hand. It was as though the effort involved in writing and all the lonely hours were too great a sacrifice for her. Perhaps if she could have used the oral tradition she studied in her classical education it might have made a difference. But she would rather *converse* (which, ironically, was her maiden name) with someone rather than write alone. It was the human factor that mattered to her. It is too bad in a way: I would not have to harvest those memories on scraps of paper to find such a person as she.

My mother, in speaking of her longevity said many times that she lived a long life because she wanted to see how it all came out, how it all ended. To leave early would be like walking out on the last act of a play or closing a book before the last chapter. There were children, grandchildren and great-grandchildren. There were old friends. There was a world, the world she might have left. There were memories to resurrect. There were things that other generations should know. There were family histories to up-date. It was up to her to make sure that everyone was still all right; that everything was still all right. Good sentinel that she was, it was still her watch and so she could not rest.

During the last few months she lived in her own home of sixty years she would ask me to take her "home." She was, of course, speaking about her childhood home in Oswego, New York. Going home had become her obsession.

"It's not far from here," she would tell me, anticipating what might be an objection. But how could I object to her wanting to come full circle, from going back to the beginning?

"I'm not sure I know the way," I told her, explaining failure in advance.

She smiled weakly. "I'll show you, dear. Please!"

And so I drove her around Delmar while she gave me directions. "Turn right," she would say. "Then the next left."

And so it went. I followed her directions for half an hour or so as we drove the familiar streets. Then her directions trailed off, came less frequently and finally stalled to silence. Then I would take her back to our starting point and without a word we would enter the house. For a while there would be a profound silence, not always the silence of failure, but sometimes the charged silence of possibility: both of us seemed to sense a feeling of having made it part way back in time—just by trying so hard.

"Perhaps next time," she would say, her voice suddenly rising on a note of hope. And then: "Perhaps we didn't look hard enough." She paused, her forehead threaded in thought. "Perhaps we didn't love enough." What she said sounded like a quotation remembered, an echo from a literary past.

I could find no answer to that benediction so I tucked it away in a corner of my mind, still another gilded footnote to her own version of the Book of Ruth.

Thunder Storms and Thunder Beings

IT was a fear that came to her in childhood. Lightning came down the chimney of her home and shot its bluish flame at her from the fireplace across the room. Up to that time the fireplace had been a warm and comfortable place, a traditional hearth and refuge from the winter cold in Northern New York State. But never again. The lightning did not strike her but she was scarred for life, scarred by the terror of what might have been and her reaction to her own active imagination. A clap of thunder accompanied the lightning bolt and so sound too was a partner in an ancient primeval conspiracy.

My mother showed fear for nothing else—except the fear of not growing old gracefully. She lived through two World Wars in which her husband-to-be and then her son served in the military. She survived a devastating influenza epidemic and, in the 30's a polio epidemic. She suffered the usual ". . . slings and arrows of outrageous fortune." She buried her kid sister who died young, as did her father. She endured what she had to and still retained her courage, faith and sense of dignity and humor. She was in control—or had the illusion of being in control. But electrical storms were inexplicable: they were nature's madness maddened! A bombardment that made no sense! An enemy to which there was no appeal.

She called on the Lord when she was so terrified. She used prayer, holy candles, statues and rosary beads to drive away the demoniac explosions from above. The storms brought about a change in her: her demeanor; a change in her chemistry as well. Suddenly she became a victim with only a prayer and a few icons for protection. At the first distant rumbles of thunder she would wake up her children and we would sit downstairs in the living room, away from the windows and the yawning fireplace. She would unplug all electrical appliances, including the lights. Then she would light the holy candles placed about the room and soon the flames, like tongues lapped the darkness with a sputtering sound. Her mouth chewed on silent prayers. Her face was frozen in a mask of anxiety. Her fingers deftly sorted beads into invisible bins. And she would sit there as quietly as possible as if not to disturb the universe or the lesser gods of storm and strife—for ten minutes, an hour or however long it took for the storm to pass.

Strangely, no one else in the family reacted as she did— with fear and trembling, not my father, my sister or my grandmother when she was visiting. And so it was painful to us, seeing her suffer that way. At various times the rest of the family tried humor, logic, scientific explanation and even a lecture on the odds against being struck by lightning. We told her (incorrectly) that lightning never struck twice in the same place. We tried to make light of her fears. But nothing worked: that early childhood experience had done its damage. She was scarred for life! Not even her faith in a benevolent God would diminish that instinctive fear over the years!

And there was another person in my life, an older man, a holy man I admired greatly. His name was Jonah and he was the native counterpart of a prophet. He was one of those who taught me to see with the eye of the heart. He was a full-blooded Lakota (Sioux) Indian from one of the reservations in South Dakota. As a holy man he had the ability to see beneath the surface of things. He was a Catholic and believed passionately in Christ and His New Testament but he was also an Indian and so believed in the world of spirits as well, especially in *WakiNyaN*, the Thunder Beings. He believed in the power of wind and storm as well as the spirits that controlled them. He believed that everything, animate and inanimate, had a spirit: he listened for the chirping of the cricket and the wild, screeching cry of the hawk and then he translated their messages as he might translate a prayer into another language and then into action. He believed in the White Buffalo Woman, the woman who brought the sacred pipe to the Lakota people. He believed no less in the Virgin Mary and the communion of saints. He straddled two worlds and took the best from each.

But Jonah grew old and lived alone in a tarpaper shack on the prairie after his wife died. He lived with loneliness, diabetes and was crippled by arthritis so that his hands were shaped like a claw, like something that crawled on the bottom of the sea. He grew sad and yearned for the old days and what might be again beyond the Spirit Trail; yearned to see his friends and relatives; yearned for the life that had been. So he called on *WakiNyaN*, the Thunder Beings. He bought a section of lightning rod at a local hardware store and soon afterwards went to church and to confession: he made his peace with God and man. Then, in the company of his closest friend he waited for the thunderheads to boil up in the West, waited to feel the static electricity in the air, waited for the sparks to ignite his blood truths. His friend drove him in his pickup truck to the foot of a butte, the very same butte where Jonah had made his Vision Quest for three days and nights without food and little water, the place he had discovered the source of his power and his new name.

But now his power had failed him, gone like his youth and strength. He was an old man being pulled to the ground by a force like gravity, a force he could not understand except to call it growing old. And so Jonah decided to leave this world on his own terms, in his own time and in his own way with the help of the Thunder Beings.

When the storm from the West finally broke over the Dakota prairie Jonah and his friend were waiting, and as the storm approached he left the pickup truck and climbed the butte as if to meet it, lightning rod held high so that he looked like a prairie Moses. The thunder broke; the lightning cracked like a whip; the rain swept over in horizontal sheets. And Jonah began singing his death song, a song silenced by the storm but recalled later by his friend:

> "*WakiNyaN*, have pity on me!
> I have lived long enough
> And want to be born again!"

Suddenly there was a blue explosion and the rod Jonah carried lit up and the old man crumpled and fell. Later, his friend, still sitting in his truck twisted in pain. He knew when it happened, he told me afterwards. There was a difference, he said: "A kind of holy happening . . ."

Not long ago I was on a commercial flight and we encountered a severe thunderstorm: passengers were asked to remain seated and fasten their seat belts. A few minutes later the Captain's calm and professional voice reassured us that he would try to get around the storm. Soon I felt the aircraft changing altitude and direction and in another five minutes the storm had faded off our wing.

The incident stirred only memory: suddenly I was back in our family's living room and we were all sitting there empathizing once again with my frightened mother. And then that scene was replaced by another. An old man in a raging storm was singing his death song, begging the Thunder Beings to release him from the bondage of this world and take him to a better world, a world he had known in his youth and imagined for a lifetime.

Two important people in my life—my mother and Jonah. One was bonded to the wilder elements by fear, the other by wonder and awe. And I, much closer to the storm center at 33,000 feet, had felt nothing at all—not fear, not wonder—just the terrible ennui of a dispassionate and weary traveler who remembered two people who *did* experience something compelling, something that changed their lives. And suddenly I felt very distant and separate from those I loved and remembered.

Part Two

Stations Along
the Way

The Doubters

ONCE, in a moment of anguish, doubt or discouragement my mother, a lifelong Catholic, confessed to me: "I never prayed so hard for anything as that it might all be true." *All* meant the promise of Christ. *All* meant the resurrection of the body, heaven, life everlasting. *All* meant reunion with loved ones in perpetual joy. *All* meant what we dared not hope before the promise of a risen Lord. *All* was a muted cry: "Lord, may it be so!"

I remember I was surprised, even shocked. Mother had never talked that way before—and she never did again. It was just one sentence in the millions we exchanged in her century on this earth. Her words took only seconds to speak and she spoke them in a near whisper but they still echo in my memory. And she was a woman of great faith who raised both her children in the faith as well.

I did not respond to her startling confession. I did not ask for an explanation or pursue the matter. I recall there was a profound silence and then the conversation turned to other things, secular and mundane. Some private crisis of faith had passed with her unexpected confession to me. I was never to know what it was. She never spoke of it again.

Later in my life I attempted to write a short story about a bishop of the future who confessed in my mother's words: "I never prayed so hard for anything as that it might all be true." In the story he had been deep in prayer when suddenly his mind went blank, his prayer crumbled and would not be supported by thoughts or words. Paralyzed by an overwhelming doubt that left him feeling guilty, weak and trembling he arranged for an immediate confession and when he had told what he considered his "sin" a great peace came over him and he returned to his duties, his conviction restored. But my story would not come—the right words were not there and I abandoned the idea. I think now that perhaps only a Graham Greene might have written that story of guilt and redemption convincingly.

Ours is a religion of hopes, promises and great expectations. A religion of faith. And yet there are doubts: our human condition would have it so. It is as though our humankind could not envision such a glorious victory as was promised, a victory over sin, death and ourselves. It is the supreme happy ending for the faithful and yet we know that we are unworthy and therefore can't even imagine a forgiveness, a grace so deep and embracing.

There have always been doubters, even among saints, men and women unable at times to get beyond their doubts—St. Thomas the Apostle, was perhaps the most humanized in the New Testament, but there were others, from Augustine to St. Francis Xavier. And St. Paul—he was crushed by doubt and disbelief until he took the road to Damascus which was also his road to faith. Peter too had his doubts, his three denials. In fact, one might wonder if a temporary and agonizing doubt is not almost a requirement for sainthood because doubt leads to reaffirmation, rededication and repentance and the redeeming words of an anguished Thomas: "My Lord and my God!"

But saints are not mothers, not usually the ones who nursed you through faith to God. Saints are not those only a heartbeat away. Not someone who can startle you with a quiet confession on the cusp of doubt, where for years there was only certainty. The lives of saints are indeed inspirational but the lives of mothers are entwined with our own in a very special way.

I have experienced those same doubts myself: you probably have too. British novelist and poet Thomas Hardy expressed our collective hope which along with faith is the most powerful antidote to doubt. In his poem, *The Oxen,* he writes of the nativity scene he imagines on Christmas Eve, the scene outside in his barn. He concludes the poem by saying that if someone asked him to go there and see for himself:

> "I should go with him in the gloom,
>   Hoping it might be so."

We want desperately to believe! We need to believe! Our hearts urge us to do so! But, at times, the mind is a stubborn opponent for it seeks the rational, the logical, the truth according to ourselves and our own limited perceptions. Mind and heart: there is frequently a conflict between the two. Love, faith and the will to believe live in the heart's precincts. The mind is adversarial and recognizes no boundaries. Imagination bounces wildly between the two. We yearn for belief, for equilibrium, for harmony. We yearn for peace—of mind, of soul. We yearn for a oneness with the object of our belief. But the mind raises doubts, challenges our beliefs, refuses to accept the fruits of our intuition, our knowing without understanding. The suspicious mind demands objective evidence and the resulting tensions are difficult to endure or resolve. The eternal struggle between the heart and the mind—it is the cargo of all humanity.

Perhaps it would be too easy if belief and faith, acceptance and harmony came too easily. If there were no struggles, nothing really to win or prove by prayer or sacrifice. If no penance was necessary. Victories have to be won by struggle: they cannot be ours by default and still kindle our faith.

These are some of the truths my mother taught me in that one-sentence confession that day long ago. And looking back on it, as I often do, she combined all the methods of a gifted teacher (which she was) into her lesson on faith. By *not* explaining, she encouraged her son to explain. By *not* explaining she planted a seed of wonder and hope in me, a seed that has grown over the passing years. She challenged me with a silence that spoke louder than words. She challenged me with what must have been a painful and secret doubt. She prepared me for my own doubts to come. And, above all, she set an example to others for overcoming doubt all the rest of her life.

If doubts are the scars on faith then we all have badges we may display as honorable and battle-won. If doubts are the wounds on belief then we all must limp along with the walking wounded. And if doubts are dangers and temptations then they are only a few of the Stations along the way. There are others to restore our belief, our faith.

Mother's Book of Hope

MY mother, then in her 97th year, kept a 50-year-old directory of her hometown, a directory containing the names, addresses, and telephone numbers of people who had once been friends and neighbors. The cover had long since fallen off, and the book was held together with two heavy rubber bands. It was stuffed with slips of paper bearing the names of those who had moved away or died. I thought of this book she always kept behind a pillow on her couch as the book of the dead, a cemetery of words.

That year, like every year, I asked if she would like a new directory, one that reflected the current town and residents.

She shook her head no, she wasn't interested in the newest edition. "This," she said, "is my book of hope."

"What do you mean, book of hope?" I asked my mother.

She smiled a faraway, secret smile. "The way it was," she said. "Once it was all that was possible."

She had not said "all there *was*," but "all that was *possible*." It was a fine but important distinction.

One day, I found her book of hope on the floor, rubber bands off and contents spilled out. I picked it up and began putting it back together. Though I looked for some principle of organization, I couldn't find one. My mother had always been a saver, unable to throw things away. And I had to admit that everything seemed to have significance: a part of the past, a part of someone's life, a random harvest of memory.

In her book of hope, I discovered a paper I had written in first grade, a picture of a friend, baseball cards, several obituaries, sugar coupons from the war, recipes clipped from magazines and newspapers, names of people and places, telephone numbers. There were scraps from the '20s, the '30s, the '40s. And there were brief messages that didn't seem to mean anything at all: "like echoes bronzed," "eight days till Sunday," "Trader Horn," "the seventh season," "angel walk." All in her own hand.

Two World Wars, a terrible Depression, and nearly a century of life. How to explain it all?

Though I couldn't put her book together again, my mother never noticed, for her book of hope had no beginning and no end.

Within her book of hope, I could see that my mother's handwriting had changed slowly, almost imperceptibly, over the years. Like an old cobweb altered by the breeze, as though she were going backward in time, learning to write again in a childish hand.

Sometimes she would call one of the numbers in her book of hope and get an electronic voice telling her it was no longer in service. Sometimes she would send a note to one of the names, and it would come back stamped *Address Unknown* or *Deceased.*

Evidence that the past was over and gone? Nothing of the kind. To my mother, it was only a temporary busy signal.

More than anything, mother's book of hope was about confidence, not in the *past* but the *future.* Great expectations. What, I wondered, could a 97-year-old look forward to? I looked for the answer in her book of hope.

My mother had always been religious, but in a private way. I think she spent many hours of her life alone with God. She liked the Stations, the dark corners, the stained-glass saints. She had a rosary of old, black wooden beads. After years of use, the black had become worn and gray. I tried to give her new beads, imported beads, beads blessed by the Pope. But she preferred the old ones that had brought the family through so many crises and hard times. Even the silver crucifix was worn from her handling, as though Jesus had been hanging there not three hours but three centuries. Even so, most of her prayers were directed toward a future she faced with courage and hope.

The future was eternity, and it was gained through *faith* and *hope*. My mother's book of hope is a book for the future as well as the past, a book of becoming, of resurrection.

My mother has authored a book to be remembered by. Some older people don't write anything down but hold things carefully in their hearts. Others find different ways to express hope: embroidery, a flower garden, painting, photography. The important thing is to begin again, to start over in some way, however simple. To do so is to affirm faith in the future and hope in being a part of it.

Because of my mother's book of hope, I began to think of my own life and my own writing as a kind of hopeful journey.

I recalled a picture that hangs in my study, a picture of young soldiers who died too young—the comrades I flew with, killed in action. I had thought of them as dead and gone, a part of my life that was over. But the book of hope, I remembered, has no chapters; it flows like time, and thus the past becomes a part of the future.

I recalled also a special box of letters, letters going back to my high school days and before. A lace Valentine that holds a special meaning. Several yellowed obituaries for those who had died too soon. All the special things that show I have been here and, like my mother, still have hope for the future.

A Tale of Two Churches

IMPLOSIONS—those violent collapses inward—are different from explosions, which are attacks from without, attacks with wrecking ball, backhoe, and sledge hammer. Implosions are to explosions as suicide is to murder. Buildings may be the most dramatic of implosions, for to watch a condemned structure collapse upon itself in a cloud of dust and debris is to witness a finality as permanent as death. And to see a building fall neatly between two standing buildings is to see high-tech efficiency in motion.

To the casual spectator, it is a show worth a few minutes of time at best. To others, the collapse seems almost sacrificial—as though the weakening walls and empty corners know somehow that it is time to make way for tomorrow. To others still, the fall of a building makes a painful separation from a living past, and all of that instant absence must be rebuilt as memory, for the architecture of so many yesterdays cannot fall victim to a single moment in time.

When I went home for a visit as a grown man, I arrived in time to witness my boyhood parish church, St. Thomas, come tumbling down into a pile of bricks and mortar—and memories, for I had made my first Communion there, had been confirmed there, had been married there. I had sung in the church choir and played on the church softball team. I had greeted new lives there and said final good-byes—ceremonies of innocence, rituals of remembrance.

As I passed by, I noticed a crowd had gathered and saw that the area around the church had been roped off and was being secured by the police. I saw construction teams and demolition equipment. I asked someone what it was all about, and he told me that the church was being demolished to make way for a new one. Moments later I heard the implosions. The sounds were far away, like distant echoes. I watched, amazed and saddened, as the four walls seemed to shiver and then fold inward, raining bricks and memories.

The charges had been well set: the house of prayer and celebration seemed to cry out for mercy and the last rites, and in moments the church that shared my birth date had fallen and was no more. It had been erased like a mistake. I said a silent prayer not only for St. Thomas but for its longtime pastor, Father H. I was thankful that he was not alive to see it turned into what now resembled a battle zone.

I looked around and saw that other longtime members of the parish were there, watching and mourning. I even recognized a few. There was Henry, the organist; Mike, who had been an altar boy; and Zack, the groundskeeper. One old woman was saying her rosary like a condemned prisoner's mother praying for a last-minute reprieve. Another wept unashamedly. A few nuns in starched habits reminded me of birds of waiting, birds of sorrow.

"I was there for the first Mass," one old man said in a shaken voice, "and I was there for the last."

"It stood for only forty years," another said, "and then the congregation outgrew it. It'll be the parking lot for the new building." "I don't believe it!" another woman kept saying over and over in a litany of doubt.

My own thoughts and emotions were just as confused as those of the other bystanders. At first I thought my passing by here had been an accident. Then I wondered whether it might be providential, fall under some plan for an old parishioner. The timing struck me as too precise for coincidence. And in the silent aftermath of the church's fall, I heard a voice say: "Unless I see the new church rise from the dust; unless I put my fingers into the place in his side, I will not believe!"

The voice of Saint Thomas, the apostle!

That evening my mother saw pictures of the demolition in the local papers. Although she had been depressed about it—so depressed that she had not even mentioned it to me in her letters or our phone conversations—she wanted to go to the place and see for herself. She told me that she could not bear to go and see the still-standing church for the last time. "But now I feel a little guilty," she confessed, "that I couldn't share in the sorrow."

The next morning I drove her to the site, explaining as we went that God's work would go on. Masses would continue, with the other parishes in the diocese taking up the slack. I explained that as the community had grown, so had the number of Catholics, and that the old St. Thomas was not able to meet the needs of the growing congregation. I told her that a new, larger, and grander church would go up on the same spot and that there were plans for a school as well. She listened and nodded, but her heart was committed to what had been.

When we arrived at the place where the church had stood, much of the rubble had been carted off and replaced with a sign announcing that a new church would be built there—a promise intended to lighten the burden of loss. My mother read the words and shook her head. "It won't be the same," she said. "Things never are."

We were there for perhaps half an hour while she sorted her memories and said her good-byes to a place she had known and loved for nearly half a century, to a congregation of friends and neighbors. Looking at her face, I could see that implosions were going on inside her and that other walls were about to come crashing down—the walls of time, the walls of memory. And as I watched, the walls did come down, but they fell without a sound. And that was the worst part. It was as though one were badly wounded yet felt no pain. Finally she asked: "The things inside? The crucifix, organ, windows, statues?"

I guessed rather than lied. "All removed; all saved to be a part of the new church." I hoped to God it was all true.

"I hope so," she echoed.

She asked me to take a picture or two, which I did. But I felt like someone trying to photograph a ghost or perhaps absence itself. After the futile picture taking, I bent down and picked up a small piece of brick and presented it to her like a holy relic. She accepted it as Veronica might have taken the veil. She seemed to weigh it in her hand, balance it on some scales of the heart. "Not much to show for all those years," she said quietly.

After that, Mother never said much about her loss. Never one to call attention to her own suffering, she was always attending to the pain of others. But I had seen what implosions could do, and her sorrow had become my sorrow. And when the new church was dedicated and consecrated, we were there.

She had driven past the construction site many times, but when the new church was completed and ready for Mass, she approached it timidly and with a certain deference, as though it were a holy stranger. Once inside, however, she recognized some familiar faces, not only in the congregation but in the artifacts. The old Stations of the Cross, seven to a side, paraded their sorrows along the walls. Statues of Mary, Joseph, and Jesus stood in timeless alabaster. Thomas and other saints walked the clouds. The altar light, the stained-glass windows, and the crucifix were all the same. Later, at Christmastime, the same nativity scene decorated the altar. And for one longtime parishioner, it was like the Easter Sunday that followed a Friday's sorrow.

My mother's funeral services were held in the Church of St. Thomas the Apostle in February 1996, and in the more than thirty years since the destruction of the old St. Thomas, my mother had made her separate peace. She had become reconciled to her loss, just as she had been reconciled to other changes in the Church. She missed the Latin Mass and kneeling at a communion rail. She missed Father H. and his homemade shrine to Our Lady. She missed the hundreds of little things that time had taken or altered. But she still remained one of the faithful, her protests mostly undetectable except to those who knew her well. But once in a while there was a certain expression, a turning inward, a silence when the congregation exploded in song, a desire to be alone in the church on a Monday—signs that time and loss had wounded her. But old people are vulnerable to churches fallen, ancient wars, and remembered faces. We all come to this point, for we are all the keepers of the kingdom of memory.

I was pleased that the priest read from the Book of Ruth, not only because my mother's name was Ruth but because, like her biblical counterpart, she was a woman of selfless love and passionate loyalty. And as the priest read Ruth's well-known poetic vow to follow her mother-in-law, Naomi: "Wherever you go I will go . . . your people shall be my people, and your God my God," a portrait of my mother emerged—a portrait of loving devotion, a woman ambushed by memory. She had come back to St. Thomas. She had come home! And under my breath, I took an aging writer's liberty and added one line to the Book of Ruth: "And your church shall be my church!"

A Family's Paper Trail

I DIDN'T make the paper trail, but I have *followed* it for most of my life with a writer's fascination. The trail was made by other family members, living and dead, people more dedicated and more informed than I. They left letters, diaries, histories, portraits, notes, receipts, tombstone tracings, war records—from the Revolution to World War II—report cards, canceled checks, laundry lists, and luncheon checks.

In order for a family to have a paper trail, it must have devoted pack rats, scholarly souls who care enough to knit the story of generations. Someone must do all the leg work, visiting the people and places central to the stories. And someone must not be frightened by the boundary between life and death, for he or she must live in two worlds at once, the past and the present. Through the eyes of the grandson, a deceased grandfather smiles.

If not for the paper trail, there are many we'd never know: my ancestor, Calvin Paige, for instance. He was born in an eastern Massachusetts town called Hardwick and went west on the Oregon Trail to the gold fields of California. He came back to Hardwick a millionaire and helped build a library and other public buildings. A street today bears his name, *our* name. I have stood at his grave, introduced myself, and thanked him. His is a story worth the telling.

There is a maternal greatgrandmother, known to me only in a faded family portrait, a woman who was very close to my mother. She was killed by a train in Oswego, New York, one blustery winter's day when she had a muffler wrapped around her head against the bitter cold. Her husband, who was gentle and kind, fought in the Civil War. In his diary, he wrote about home and things of beauty. The darker side, however, the suffering and death of that terrible conflict, he kept in the shadows.

There were others. A great uncle Gene was an adventurer and a soldier of fortune who traveled the world. From the stories I have heard and read, I could have written ten books about his life and times. Today, I have a book of his poetry and his sword.

Because of the paper trail, I can see my parents in a new light. I know that my mother was our family's paper trail pioneer. She saved everything as if she would live forever! A paper, handwritten, perhaps a boy's first-grade composition, was to her part of the writer, a treasure that could not be thrown away. She saved homemade valentines and baseball cards and notes from little girls who thought they loved me for a day or a week. And when my mother died, she left a paper trail a lifetime long. It is not only a legacy of remembrance, but a testament of pain. There is pain as well on the paper trail.

Along the paper trail, I have found letters from my father when he was with the American Expeditionary Force in World War I. And the diary his father had asked him to keep. They contain words addressed not only to his loved ones, but to future generations, words that have outlived him now by nearly half a century.

Along the paper trail, I also found my father's writings on the Civil War. Behind his perceptive words about Shiloh and Gettysburg, I saw the sensitive side of a man who laughed most of the time and was known primarily for his athletic ability. Almost as an antidote to the seriousness, I found among these writings the joke books he used when he acted as master of ceremonies at various social events. No matter what, you'll find surprises and contradictions along the paper trail.

Where does the trail lead? What dead end or spiritual geography do we discover there? And what do we do with all that paper? What library, museum, warehouse, human heart, or memory will hold it all? What bold technology or virtual intelligence will store it?

Does it lead to a cremation—a bonfire of memories? Perhaps. But before the burning, there will be greater knowing, even greater loving.

Someone will rediscover ancient clues . . . someday. There is always evidence left behind. Someone will dig up the arrowhead, reclaim the broken toy. Someone will find the rose pressed in the Bible at the Book of Ruth. Years and years from now, things will turn up at auctions and flea markets and garage sales. You can find them every day in the corners of drawers, boxes, and chests.

Someone will catch them once again, by accident or design. And in the shock of recognition, that someone will see the way to yesterday.

Echoes of a Lost Sunday

DURING the last five years of my mother's illness, I noticed a change in her use of language. A Latin teacher, she knew grammar well and spoke in a cultured voice with a high degree of precision. But after her 90th year, she spoke differently—and in a kind of high and tragic poetry. . . .

She was telling me one day about her childhood and how on Sunday mornings her family would go to the cemetery after Mass. There her ancestors, those she had met and those who were just names attached to a sepia photograph, slept under the shelter of the angel Gabriel's outstretched wings.

The names on the headstones became real people as her father led the prayers for the repose of their souls, reciting each name in a ceremony of inclusion. Whether they died in the Civil War or never took their first steps, they still belonged in the family circle.

Suddenly she stopped in the middle of her story and cocked her head to one side.

"What is it?" I asked. "Do you hear something?"

"Echoes," she said softly, with an approving smile. "Echoes of a lost Sunday."

I remember reading in a publication of the Alzheimer's Association that one of the warning signs of the disease was "problems with language." The article went on to say: "A person with Alzheimer's may forget simple words or use inappropriate words, making speech incomprehensible."

That definition—for the most part—was consistent with my own observations. But my experience with dementia was personal, not medical.

I visited nursing homes frequently and, once there, listened more than I spoke. I felt the experts might be missing something in their evaluations. Often, I did not find my mother's language "incomprehensible" at all. It was oblique and paradoxical, full of images and metaphors, but it was not incomprehensible. To me it had the startling language of modern poetry, and it often cut with a blade of truth.

Sometimes when I spoke with my mother, I got the feeling she was desperately trying to tell me something in a code I couldn't break. Perhaps I had to be closer to the other side before the light would shine as it did for her. It was as though we were God's spies, she and I—God's spies on a secret mission—and her language reflected this.

Sometimes, her language sparkled like jewels under a light. Looking around the house, full of everything but family, she said, "How empty the emptiness with everyone gone. . . ."

Another time, addressing my deceased father's picture: "How empty of me to be so full of you."

Once she referred to her condition in the nursing home as being ". . . adrift on confinement." And seeing out the window red and gold leaves waltzing earthward, ". . . the big, little deaths of autumn." Still later, in her attempt to find the part of her that was lost, she said: "All that was me is gone."

"Hope is the thing with feathers," wrote Emily Dickinson, "that perches in the soul. . . ." And while most agree that Dickinson's professional skill did not match her poetic vision, her insights and perceptions—in spite of simplistic stanzas—were among the most powerful in American poetry.

It is not only Emily Dickinson who shows the resemblance between the language of the "lost" and the exalted language of the artistic. The more "modern" poet, Wallace Stevens, wrote phrases like ". . . when the sky is so blue, things sing themselves . . ." and "He knew that he was a spirit without a foyer . . ."

Countless examples can be taken from modern poets and compared with the voices of people speaking the language of a secret hope or pain, the urgent language of *nostalgia*, a Greek word meaning "to look back in pain."

Other words from my mother struck me by their beauty, insight, or clarity

"How many heartbeats to a life?"

". . . God's arms are full of broken things . . ."

". . . crying in a minor key . . ."

". . . losing myself to time . . ."

". . . caught in funnels of sunshine . . ."

". . . smooth as glass in the tides . . ."

". . . renting from God . . ."

The images may be of pain or joy, doubt or security—but they are powerful by any literary standard. They stop us in our reading like a roadblock on the highway. They demand our attention, guiding us like prayer itself.

I cannot explain *why* the language of those suffering from dementia is this way. It may be that they are closer to the other side, closer to what my mother sometimes referred to as the influence of the "Blue Lady." I cannot explain why those whose speech is often labeled "inappropriate" or "incomprehensible" can be sometimes crystal clear.

Some will probably say it is not a conscious effort at communication. They will say it is a reflex action, that words just float to the surface of consciousness like sunken things released from the bottom of a muddy pond.

I have no answers, but I am glad I heard the words. They helped me to understand the possibilities of language. They helped me become a translator of suffering and of those who speak in the most elusive of tongues.

I sometimes borrowed that special language and used it for my own, trying to capture what ordinary language would not. I owe a debt to those who speak the language of paradox and pain. Those who speak in code and invite me to join. I also owe a debt to all those "echoes of a lost Sunday" that resound in memory's hushed canyons. And I thank them all for the language that has risen higher than words, just as music can rise beyond sound.

The Strength of Cobwebs

"COBWEBS are stronger than steel," my mother told me once and it has taken more than half a century for me to understand what she meant.

My mother, was a great person, a great soul, but she was never, by her own admission, a great housekeeper. There were too many other things that were more important to her—visiting with family and friends; playing bridge; reading books and accompanying her husband and son on their rounds of summer tennis tournaments. She was a people-person. And so, as a result of her priorities, I grew up in a house festooned with cobwebs fluttering like torn veils in the corners of things.

Now I do not know if cobwebs must be spun by spiders or if they can be spun by time, dust and neglect as well. It does not matter much, I guess: the important thing is that they are there and growing, wafting in the slightest breeze and sometimes breaking loose and floating like gossamers . . .

At first I recall them as objects of fear, making strange shapes and moving shadows. Especially around Halloween time when the mindset was ghosts, haunted houses and things cobwebby. After a child's nightmare too they seemed to move like nets to catch and hold a fear. And sometimes they seemed like dream objects, as fragile as dreams themselves. As insubstantial too.

Sometimes they served to bind together things that seemed to have little in common. A tennis trophy and the statue of an unknown saint; a model airplane and a Latin dictionary. A wish and a memory. Sometimes they bind things together in a visual paradox.

There were times when, on impulse, I swept them away with a broom, but that was a mistake: I found that I grew to miss them. They had added something somehow—something like atmosphere or ambiance to a boy's ordinary room filled with college pennants, pictures of sports' heroes and suspended model airplanes. They added *character*, like dust to a bottle of rare wine in a wine cellar. Or a white beard on a very old man. And, every once in a while I thought of them as guy wires, holding things together—although at the time, I didn't know *what* things. But the time was 1939 and the world beyond my four corners had begun to fall apart.

When war finally came to America I thought of my cobwebs as safety nets: something to catch me should I fall. Or should I stray too far beyond the point of no return. I had enlisted in the Army Air Forces and was waiting to be called into active service. Now, in my dreams and reveries I could see myself as an "ace" in war-torn skies. Sometimes I could see my plane being shot down and I could see myself falling, tugging at the ripcord of a parachute that wouldn't open. And, after a long and terrifying free-fall, at the very last moment, I found myself in the safety of a net—a net that was familiar, dark and silky.

And when I was far away from home I thought about those cobwebs often and they seemed to bind me to all it was I was missing—a *place* unique in memory, and I remember thinking how I wished they were visible and stirring like ensigns, battered and torn yet still flying after a battle.

And they *were* still there when I returned. I got the strange feeling that those cobwebs in my old room had been spared the broom deliberately and for some special reason—something that was a part of my homecoming. Something as important as a home-cooked meal or seeing everyone again.

Later, when I returned for a visit with children of my own, my old room was where one of them stayed. I noticed the cobwebs had been swept away, the room painted. And I was truly sorry I didn't have to answer questions about those dark, scary things hanging from the ceilings and in the corners. I was sorry because I had a heart full of good answers.

But, in time, the cobwebs returned, growing like hanging scarves, moving to the almost imperceptible currents that even a breath might make. And, for a while, things were almost the same again.

My father's stroke put him in my old room and he stayed there until it was time for him to go to the Veterans' Hospital, a place he never left alive. More than once I found him studying those cobwebs in the corners as though they were the scrawling signatures of Time. He was caught by their motion, held by the memories they spun. And, later, in the VA hospital I found him searching the corners of his antiseptic room for a familiar tapestry of motion, a signal, an invitation to remember.

I watched my mother grow old under those cobwebs that spanned the corners like a bridge to yesterday. And yet I did not sweep them down. I started to a few times before I realized that it wasn't cleanliness that was next to godliness: it was *connectedness*.

Later the house was put up for sale. And, in anticipation of the visits of real estate agents and assorted strangers, the cobwebs would be swept down, the house made ready. Commerce will do what Time would not; what memory would not; what I would not . . .

"Cobwebs are stronger than steel."

I don't really remember how long ago my mother said those words. I know it has been a long time, over fifty years, maybe even longer. I don't recall the circumstances that prompted her to say a thing like that either. It wasn't the sort of thing that capped a casual conversation. But it was her way to come out with sudden and cryptic sentences that were both a challenge and a delight. She said things that were unexpected: she strung words together like jewels on a necklace. She said things you might remember after fifty or sixty years—like those quotable passages from the Bible or Shakespeare. Once in a while there was a paradox hidden in the things she said: the sentences didn't seem to make sense until you took them apart and then put them together again. As with something mechanical. And then the meaning would suddenly become apparent in a burst of recognition. Some of my mother's sentences were learning experiences in themselves.

Not long ago at a crafts fair I saw what I thought were cobwebs holding a colorful feather, but, on closer inspection I saw that they were Dream Catchers, those popular Native American circular webs of leather designed to keep the bad dreams out of our consciousness. According to the small brochure dangling from them, they were supposed to be hung next to one's bed where they would act as a filter for nightmares and let only the sweet dreams through. I bought two or three and hung them in the corners of my bedroom where they still remind me of another time, another house and the cobwebs that shifted with all the strange motions and currents.

My mother said that cobwebs were stronger than steel and, for me, they have proved to be. For they have served as nets, webs, tapestries, guys, ties and bonds. They have held many things together and fashioned their own memories. And, to me, those who see them as the work of spiders or unsightly things the broom has missed just don't understand the strength of cobwebs and how they are related to time and memory.

Later my mother spoke another sentence that startled me with its poetic insight. She said suddenly, and in a tone of reverie: "Yes, I do remember now that there was such a person as I." And for a moment there was a tight fist closing on my heart. I knew what she meant. She was thinking of the good days, the days before the fog came between her and the world. When things were as they appeared to be. When we were all young and together. The days of Self and satisfaction . . .

But time has passed, a river of time and we were together, but separately, she in her world, I in mine.

I had to grow old myself to understand what my mother meant by her remark about the strength of cobwebs. I had to grow into a painful kind of wisdom. There are no shortcuts. I think of this period as my second life: we all have them. We all go around twice, once in youth and again in age.

Every once in a while in my older man's bedroom I notice the beginnings of a delicate cobweb reaching for one of the adjacent Dream Catchers. I look for a spider, but see none. I watch, fascinated, as it sways in the corner like a broken trapeze swinging between Now and Then . . .

The Democratic Aristocrat

MY mother was, in many ways, aristocratic: she believed in an aristocracy, not of wealth, power or title, but of goodness, intelligence, compassion and sensitivity. She believed that some people had more to give to the world than others by virtue of their intelligence, passion, abilities or dedication. It was more than *noblesse oblige* for she believed that such potential benefactors had a God-given responsibility to share their blessings with others.

Although her French Canadian father was a small town grocer and not a wealthy or powerful man, he was a *good* man, often extending credit to help his customers, even to the extent of jeopardizing his own business. He was a man who provided a college education to his two daughters in a time when males were usually given preference in education. My mother was born into this working class environment, into the world of small business and small town living. Yet, all the while she must have been dreaming a classical dream of Rome and Athens and golden ages long past.

She did have an aristocratic bearing and demeanor: not much over five feet, she carried herself regally except for later in her life when she was fighting gravity. She also had an accent that could not be traced to Northern New York State: her accent was not of place so much as culture. She spoke a formal English and a formal French, devoid of slang or vulgarity. Her vocabulary was large and she used words that were not a part of popular speech, words like *indubitably, identic, valiant* and *myriad*, words that others sometimes thought obscure. Her diction was like that of an actress in a classical drama no matter who her audience might be. Never patronizing, she paid everyone the compliment of her best.

Yet she could not ". . . suffer fools gladly." She showed great patience with the young, the slow or the ignorant but little with pretenders to wisdom or those who considered themselves superior without justification. And she had little patience with the intellectually lazy. She was a natural teacher but she made certain assumptions as well as demands on those she instructed, including her children. She taught them to be confident of their abilities but never to betray what they had been given. "Remember," she would tell us, "you didn't make yourself. What you have in the way of blessings are gifts from God and the teachings of others." And her familial loyalties were almost tribal in their passion and intensity.

In her relations with strangers she tended to be formal and civil, her civility based on her recognition of the innate dignity and worth of every individual. The town drunk or the retarded she treated exactly as she would treat the town supervisor or the bank president. In a time of segregation and thinly disguised prejudice she showed none. Perhaps that was because, as one of the few Catholics in a largely Protestant suburb she had known prejudice herself. I still remember how we went to Mass in a private home because there was as yet no Catholic church in town. Yet mother was proud of her Catholicism and proud too of the sacrifices necessary in order to practice her faith and raise her children in it. She hoped it might be an inspiration to those who had known the prejudice of others. Reserved and unemotional in public, my mother did not wear her heart upon her sleeve, but, at times, there were tears on her sleeve. Beneath her stoical manner there was a fine-tuned sensibility. To those who did not know her well she frequently seemed aloof, even unapproachable, but that was not the case: she was vulnerable and easily wounded. And she was warm and sympathetic when there was the need to be.

My mother's younger sister was said to be the beauty in the family and my mother was regarded as the "smart" one. All throughout her life she considered herself "plain." "I'm pretty," she would say with the ghost of a smile, and then add: "Pretty homely and pretty apt to stay that way." But, behind her careless dismissal there was a pain that webbed her face, the pain of a woman who confused physical beauty with a richer beauty. She spent little money on cosmetics or beauty preparations. She would use the same tube of lipstick for years, the same face powder and rouge. But, if the old adage that beauty is in the eyes of the beholder is true then she lived in the reflected beauty of many. And I thought that when she was very old and close to death her beauty was the greatest, as a candle flame burns brightest just before it goes out.

My mother loved my high school friends and our home was one of the few meeting places in a time when community centers, town parks and public swimming pools and skating rinks were not to be found. My mother opened her home and her heart to my friends of the Class of '40, to those who in another year would be leaving for war and coming to say good-bye. And then there would be homecomings too as they would return to visit when they were on leave before they shipped out. They called her "Ma," not her favorite appellation but one that touched her in a special way. "All my sons," she would call them and when one did not return from Guadalcanal or Iwo Jima or the skies over Europe there was a loss that was registered in the depth of her eyes.

Beneath her outward confidence and courageous mien there was great uncertainty and fear, not for herself but for others, especially family. Her first question whether speaking over the telephone or in person was: "Is everything all right?" And, of course, *everything* also included *everyone*. And I feel certain that she asked the same question in her prayers.

If everything was all right—then God was in His heaven and all was right with the world. For her world spun on a fragile axis and traveled in a narrow orbit. What she feared most was caprice, chance, contingency and all those other words that mean the accidental and the unpredictable. Such concepts horrified her and were the greatest challenges to both reason and her faith. *Things* might go wrong, but *people* were watched over by God and angels and were more than sparrows. On that point she quoted the saints and Albert Einstein who proclaimed: "God does not play dice with the universe."

As a result of all her qualities, including her paradoxes and contradictions, my mother, democrat and aristocrat, had a mysterious, even intriguing, aura about her that might set a person to wondering if she might not be a famous author living *in cognito* or perhaps she might be a European of royal descent, stolen by gypsies and brought to America. But no—she needed no romanticized fiction to explain her. She was just a small town girl from Northern New York, a girl with a good mind and a big heart. A girl who dreamed big dreams and then tried her best to live them. With her family's help she graduated from college, married her soldier back from war, raised a loving family and served her God. And most of it was good, except for the ending. But that too is problematic. Her first question when she arrived in heaven was undoubtedly: "Is everything all right?" And then she added: "On earth?"

And Paradise itself depended on the answer . . .

A Calendar Page

IT was a page torn from a century of an old woman's life, perhaps from time itself. It was a calendar page from the month of October in the year 1974 and the space beneath the 10th day was filled in with the name *Monte* in my mother's bold hand. Monte was her husband and our father and October 10, 1974 was the day of his death. There was nothing else written on that calendar page: it was as though time had stopped on the 10th. And so it did for one much loved husband and father: the end of earthly time, the beginning of eternity.

The calendar page was found among our mother's "things" after her own death, twenty-two years after Monte's. Her "things" included anything and everything that might be stored in drawers or cardboard cartons boldly marked "Save!" so that my sister and I might examine the contents and make our own judgments on the contents. But the apple doesn't fall all that far from the tree: we were her grown children and so judged as she might have judged. Not surprisingly, we decided to save and preserve, even as moth and rust came ever closer.

My sister often said that our home should have become a museum, that things should never have to be thrown out, but rather preserved for an unknown posterity. But such is not the world's way: life is not a hoarder but more the profligate. Auctions, even the popular garage sales were never a possibility with our mother. The vulturism of strangers bartering in the driveway—it would have been unthinkable. And what, she might have asked, was the price of memories and souvenirs from a time long gone? How much was my first crystal set worth? My baseball cards? My sister's first doll? Our First Communion kits from Mama, our beloved maternal grandmother? No, such things did not come with a price tag nor could one be arbitrarily placed on them.

And then there were the words! Many of the cardboard cartons were filled with words—words in the form of notes, letters, newspaper clippings, recipes, cryptic messages and even laundry lists. To mother the written word was sacred, something permanent, engraved in stone. As much a part of a person as flesh and blood, DNA or fingerprints. To throw away someone's words was to throw away a part of the person—like burning his letters or possessions. Or, in the case of letters, taking a piece of his heart. And so the cardboard boxes were filled one by one, filled with words from the living and the dead, all randomly boxed with no arrangement, system, rhyme or reason. And so, from an early age my sister and I learned that words were not only the keys to ideas and the magical world of books but they were shields to protect against the silent times.

For hadn't our father, Monte, spent his last year in silence? Hadn't he said nothing in all those days and nights in the Veterans Hospital? Hadn't he left without so much as a good-bye? I suspect he was silent because there was nothing more to say: his life had said it all and death was still a silent stranger who sat in the corner and waited. Hadn't Monte said it all that day before the great silence came between us like a shadow? The three of us had gathered around his hospital bed and I tried to cheer him up with words. "Look, Dad," I said with a forced enthusiasm, "we're all together again."

He looked up at us from pale sheets and his eyes were the eyes of a wounded bird raised to the skies. "Yes," he said in a faraway voice, "but we're together separately."

I shall never forget those words and think of them as his last words before the great silence and because they summed up the tragedy of the human condition so perfectly.

"Yes, but we're together separately . . ." It was a legacy of sorts, like Hamlet's *". . . the rest is silence."*

We inherited boxes of cryptic messages as well, fragments and half-completed thoughts. It was almost as if she hoped that those who came after would be forced to translate and perhaps even complete them.

". . . a language not my own."

". . . a translation of echoes."

". . . the measure of memory."

". . . credences of a lost summer."

". . . reflections in a shallow dream."

". . . .translated from the silence."

". . . eight days till Sunday."

It was a secret language full of symbol and paradox, perhaps to hide a loneliness or private sorrow. It was a language she would only partially share with those who might come to decipher and try to understand sometime.

I feel certain that she thought of herself as the Keeper of the Flame: her mission in life was to keep the family safe and together and to stoke the fires of hope. It was, of course, an impossible task. She was a martyr of the moment, and like all living martyrs she must be consumed.

She left a house and a home to my sister and me and although we could not live in it, we could not live outside it either. For the most part it was a home of joy and laughter and good times. It was a house of life, a house of breath. And, if it was not possible to turn our home into a museum it *was* possible to tear it down so that no one else would ever occupy it, so it would end with the family, preserved in the dignity of oblivion.

I remember reading of a case in which a woman of almost one hundred left instructions that the family home be demolished after the death of its last member. Perhaps selfishly, perhaps lovingly, she wished no one else to live in it. It was like the breaking of the glass after the most sacred toast. But New York State preservationists had classified the old woman's home as having historical significance. And so the conflict ended up in the surrogate court where the judge ruled in favor of the owner. The house would be torn down, the city having the option of buying the empty lot for its own use. Nostalgia and heartbreak had won over history! The city *did* buy the property, black-topped it and turned it into a parking lot. And somewhere an old woman smiled at the ghost home she had saved for those who had lived in it and loved it.

I considered such an option. A home was a place of arrivals and departures, temporary at best as human beings measure time. Our family had spent the best years of our lives there. I had left for college, left for war from there. I had planted trees as memory bearers and buried secret treasures in the back yard. I had planted memories, memories that now almost touched the sky. My grandmother had died in an upstairs bedroom and that was enough to make it a holy place. Yes, demolition seemed a viable option. But then I thought that with the residual love that still was there it might become haunted—haunted with the good times, laughter and memories. Happiness might be contagious, gloriously alive with all those yesterdays. There could be a birth, a recovery, a miracle. . . No, absence wasn't the answer. Nor demolition. And then in the spring of the year after that cold February when my mother joined Monte, the question was finally put to rest, resolved by what I feel was her intervention and a living memory . . .

I was driving past our home in that time between winter and spring when I saw my mother's favorite perennials breaking through the crust of a winter past—the delicate things that bordered the driveway and the picket fence—the crocuses, the daffodils, jonquils and tulips. The first born of the winter dead! A resurrection of sorts!

I stopped, pulled into the driveway for a closer look, sure that it must be a sign. A sign that life came from death, joy from sorrow, spring from winter and today from all our yesterdays. Our mother had had the last floral expression of her will. The last word!

As I sat there in the driveway of what had been our home my imagination stirred and somehow caressed what Abraham Lincoln had called "...the mystic chords of memory." Our mother and a random selection of flowers breaking winter's crusty grip had decided the matter and suddenly I was only a witness to a greater truth.

I began these reflections with a page from a calendar, a page with the single word *Monte* on it. That page from October, 1974 still hangs over my desk as I write these words, a constant reminder that sorrow and leaving may narrow the focus of time itself so that the remaining days become as anonymous as ancient grave stones, row on row. But, just as that single word, *Monte*, may open the flood gates from which may flow remembrance, love and requiem so a scattering of perennial driveway flowers may remind us that there are other comings, other springs. Even other Octobers. And that the most important things like love and memory have no endings, but only resurrections.

Ringing Home

MY mother, on those rare occasions when the family was away from home, would ring our empty house just to listen to the sound of the phone. For her, it was like playing a musical instrument and then listening to the replay. She found it melodic and reassuring. "Everything is all right," she would announce as though she had just talked to a caretaker.

Years later, when she was widowed, she continued the practice, calling from wherever she happened to be. And even now, as she approached her 100th year, she called from her nursing home. She gave the nurse the number, and the nurse dialed and handed my mother the telephone. My mother listened to the sound of ringing in an empty house, the same sound she has heard since 1938, and a connection was made again.

I think that the ringing took my mother back to when the house was really a home, so alive you might think it had a pulse.

Then the house was almost empty, waiting to be sold.

Why telephone when there is no one to answer? Connections. Because none of us lives in the present alone. Because there are ghosts that are not only friendly but necessary in our lives.

We had no answering machine attached to our telephone. We have never had one. The phone may ring once or 50 times without interruption, as the caller dictates. My mother could listen to the same ringing she first heard almost 60 years ago.

Under memory's benevolent inspiration, she could listen once again to a daughter calling from college, to a husband away on business, to a son in military service. She could listen to phantom voices telling of grandchildren born, friends passed away, weddings being planned. She could hear big talk or small talk from a half-century ago.

Once when she called from the nursing home, I had just entered my mother's house to take care of some routine affairs. I was startled to hear the ringing of the telephone, and surprised to hear my mother's voice asking, "Who is it?" when I answered. There was as much hope in her voice as surprise.

"It's Harry," I told her. "I'm at home."

I knew what her next question would be: "Is everything all right?"

"Everything's fine, Mom," I told, her. "Just fine."

In my mind's eye, I could see her reaching for my hand as she sat in her wheelchair.

"Is everybody there?" she asked.

"All present and accounted for," I told her.

She closed with an invitation to come see her soon.

The odds against it were astronomical, but she had called what should have been an empty house and had made a connection, a loving connection. Tomorrow and the day after, she would try again, hoping to find something lost, or a familiar voice.

I suppose calling an empty house is like writing yourself a letter. It helps sometimes. It gives you a chance to create your own confidant or confessor.

Who's to answer when a phone rings in an empty house? The years will answer. All our yesterdays.

Some might describe my mother's house as an attic exploded— with its magazines from the '20s and '30s, its jars of pennies, its swelling balls of tinfoil saved for the war effort, its yellow newspaper clippings. My mother's house is a random harvest of memories.

And for me, my mother will always be the high priestess of memory, who holds lives together. She will always be the custodian of the place and its memories.

As her son, I have inherited her memory gene and her saving gene. I too sift memories from yesterdays, saving letters, notes, even scraps of paper. I too save coins in a jar.

And sometimes, when the mood is right, I even ring up my boyhood home. Love always answers the phone, even when nobody's there.

A Mother's Song

IN 1996, for the first time in a hundred years, my mother did not spend Christmas at home. She was in a nursing home, lost in time and space, retreating ever farther from herself. Within sight of neither shore, she drifted with the tides that now moved her life.

The corridor was busy with visitors carrying packages and wearing smiles over a visible sadness. I found her in the Sunshine Room, sitting in her wheelchair and looking out over the folds of snow that draped and softened the edges of the building that enveloped her. I couldn't imagine what she might be thinking as she sat there watching the courtyard fill up with east. Perhaps it was nothing at all.

There were colorful holiday decorations all around, and piped carols floated through the halls. I noticed that my mother was wearing a pin on her heavy sweater, an angel with a broken wing. Something she had won at bingo perhaps, like the four-inch figurine of the bluebird of happiness sitting on her window ledge next to all her family pictures— her gallery of yesterday.

She looked smaller to me, more fragile than she had at my last visit only two weeks earlier. With each of my visits, she seemed to shrink a little more.

When my mother recognized me, she extended her hand and I took it. A kiss was too tenuous for her, too fragile; she had to grip what it was she loved. For a moment or two she took in her surroundings, and then, with a puzzled look, asked: "Is today different?"

"It's Christmas," I told her.

Her brow knit in concern. "The same one? The one that used to be?"

I thought for a moment before I answered. "It's Christ's birthday again," I told her. It was the most innocuous answer

I could give. In places where speech between people was an effort, I found that spoken words could sometimes be like daggers, double-edged and dangerous.

I recalled that during my last visit, she had suddenly asked me once again: "Harry, would you fly me home?" It had been a strange request. My mother had never flown in her lifetime, and I had long since given up piloting planes in the military. But her question seemed to have depths of meaning. Yes, I told her, I would fly her home someday. It was a vague answer, yet honest enough to satisfy her. *Words* were sometimes sheathed by love .

In the silence that followed, I gave her a present, a shawl to help protect her from the drafts that coursed through the halls of the first floor. I draped it around her thin shoulders.

"It's always so cold in here," she complained.

"This should help," I told her.

When my mother nodded off to sleep for a few minutes, I noticed that everyone—visitors, staff, and residents—was making heroic efforts at normalcy. Things seemed familiar enough: the carols, the surrounding family members, the warm greetings, the festive decorations— what we call the "Christmas spirit." But the effect was different somehow: the whole had suddenly become less than the sum of its parts.

Outside, the clouds parted, and a burst of sun shone through. Then the clouds closed again, eclipsing the brightness. The residents noticed when the sun poured over them, and they reacted to the familiar warmth as if it were the touch of an old friend or a kiss. They lost interest when the shadows spread over the snow like a dark sundial.

My mother awoke as suddenly as she had fallen asleep. She looked around, once more aware of her surroundings. I could tell that she was again in the present; there was a difference. Staying in the present, though, was difficult, almost like walking a tightrope. For most of the residents the past was the well where the healing waters had gathered. Yet one dared not drink too deeply. There were dangers: a cold that was never very far from pain and a depth that challenged even memory. Sometimes it was better to suffer the thirst.

Some children carrying gifts came bounding down the corridor and settled around a wheelchair. Their soprano voices and bursts of activity not only brought a dozen or so heads to an erect position but caused some smiles as well. *Even now there were beginnings,* I told myself. In such a place, there weren't many, God knows—except in the endings. Mostly there was waiting, a kind of palpable and numbing wait that overshadowed almost every other activity. The residents, mostly old women, lined up like winter birds on a wire and waited for whatever came next. They began to gather a few at a time, and then they waited. They waited to get up in the morning and to go to bed at night. They waited for food trays, Mass, bingo, letters, therapy, visitors, and painkillers. They dozed while waiting for their sleeping pills. Sleep was the great escape, almost a rehearsal for eternity. And there was always the final wait for the miraculous birth that they were certain was coming.

You learned to speak in the present tense after a while. You used more gestures, a sort of sign language for the things that might hurt too much to put into words. A nod to the southwest meant home, the one she loved and had to leave. A glance down a corridor meant let's go back to your room now. An arm thrust in a sleeve meant it's time to be going. A kiss meant good-bye. It could mean *forever* . . .

At the ten o'clock Mass, I sat on the floor next to my mother, still in her wheelchair. She wore a pained yet knowing expression on her face, as though she were giving birth to a secret . . . as though she understood something for the first time . . . as though she were out of her body, an observer, a spectator. I sensed that she was in another world, one with a boundary I couldn't cross. I looked around at all the others—the old, the waiting—and it was I who felt like the stranger.

At Communion time the priest and his ministers threaded their way through the maze of wheelchairs, walkers, and bodies seated on the floor. A Savior was born again today, and the old people were hungry for his love, his help, and his mercy. They snatched at the hosts bird-like, and then their heads dropped as though they had suddenly become too heavy to support.

Minutes later the priest was singing "Silent Night," urging the congregation to join in. The first few rows of old ladies seemed to be the choir, those who knew the words and could carry a tune. The others just seemed to be chewing on a melodic memory. But the priest's enthusiasm was contagious. I even found myself singing softly, suddenly feeling a swelling of joy that I could not explain. I reached over to my mother's wheelchair and put my hand on hers.

Now I had never heard my mother sing, not once in my life. Not a popular tune or a hymn, not even so much as "Happy Birthday." She seemed to like music when it came from others, but for her it was a feeling, not a sound. But suddenly at this Christmas Mass, when she was nearly a century old, she began to sing! Singing with the choir! A miracle of sorts! Her voice was soft and rusty, as though she had not spoken for a long time and had suddenly discovered her voice, as though it was her swan song too, more beautiful because it was her last.

I nodded at her, squeezed her hand, and between us there was music. And for me, that moment has become one of time's jewels and the sound of memory itself.

Old, discouraged, homeless, heavily sedated, hurting, and suffering from some dementia, *she had sung for the first time!* Christmas Mass in that place of loneliness and secret sorrows was a revelation to me, a celebration not only of a birthday but of the human spirit as well. It suddenly struck me that these old folks were heroes, and no one even suspected. And the Lord's birthday had been the inspiration for my mother's song: her own gift to a Lord, her "Happy Birthday" at last. To a son, too, perhaps. Even as she was making her painfully slow exit from life, she was still the teacher, still the mother. Lessons in living; lessons in leaving. For her, probably for the first time in her long life, fortune no longer made hostages of her feelings, her voice.

Late in the afternoon I wheeled her back to her room. In an hour or so, darkness would fall, and she would be afraid. If she awoke in the night and called out, no one might be there. She would return to some yesterday when she was a child, to some fear of the dark that now made me afraid for her as well.

I sat by her bed and watched her drift away to the only peace she knew. Outside, the setting sun sent a few last rays through her window and across the ledge where she kept all that was left of home. It was her altar filled with her own burnt offerings. For a moment the falling rays rested on her figurine, the bluebird of happiness, ice-blue, wings folded, yet without my mother's song or promise of flight.

Beacons of Light

FOR years now I have loved lighthouses, both their form and their function. Rising tall and slender on land's end, they seem to look anxiously yet stoically seaward, like a sailor's wife on her widow's walk. And when there was a crisis or a shipwreck or people were in danger, the tower and its beacon would slice the night in warning and perhaps in rescue. I have loved lighthouses for what they were as well as for what they have become—now mostly anachronisms, tourist attractions, or historical points of interest. Now, in all their silent splendor, they seem only sentinels, guardians of a romantic past, gone but certainly not forgotten.

By inclination and temperment I might have been a lighthouse keeper. I have more than a little resistance to change in routine and lifestyle. I enjoy solitude. I prefer the familiar and am not a traveler. I feel certain that the sudden surges of adventure that the keeper's life afforded would be sufficient to hold off boredom. And even if physical action did not come, there would be time for contemplation, reading, writing, and parenting. Like Thoreau, I would travel much on my rocky or sandy beach and would come to know my barren world. There would also be that world of the moon-plagued tides and especially the world of imagination existing within the space of my own skull.

I once had an opportunity to buy a lighthouse on the Saint Lawrence River, but it was too expensive for a professor and wanna-be watcher of the tides and soaring gulls. It was one of twenty or so lighthouses on the Seaway Trail not too far from my Northern New York home and was priced at more than a half million dollars. Some lucky private citizen came up with the money and now lives among past glories and modern comforts.

Except for my proximity to the Seaway Trail and a great admiration for *Moby Dick,* I claim no seafaring influences unless there is a "lighthouse" gene, for my mother grew up in the shadow of the Oswego West Pierhead lighthouse in Oswego, New York. Nevertheless, I claim no sailor relatives. I never lived near the sea, nor did it flow in my blood.

I think I became a lover of lighthouses because of an accidental discovery that I made when I returned from military service after World War II. It was then that I learned from a neighbor and wartime air-raid warden that my mother had kept the porch light and the light in my bedroom window burning for all the days of my absence—much to the consternation of those assigned to enforce blackouts in the unlikely event enemy planes were overhead. While I was in the skies she had turned on landing lights and left them on for the duration. I had known she had said prayers and made novenas and a mother's sacrifices for me, but I had not known that she had lighted the runways and kept her vigil of light as she had done when I was younger. I am certain that I never came home to a darkened house, no matter what time of night it was. Keeping the light on was a maternal affair, a family affair, an important part of our lifestyle. Let there be light!

I never told my mother that I knew what she had done, for I thought I might embarrass her—not as much for her motherly concerns during wartime as for my discovery of her secret. And so for the three years I was away, the lights burned as prayerfully at home as those holy candles she had lighted near the altar at St. Thomas Church—a fire dance to illumine those distant runways and the darkness of her own doubts. Lighting the votive candle was her substitute for a "wing and a prayer" to keep a son airborne, a mother's defense against the Ides of March and the capricious gods of war. And, at least in our immediate family, there were no wartime wrecks. The lighthouse had worked its magic.

I remember also some magic of my own. It was during my pilot's training in Camden, Arkansas, and we cadets had been called out with torches and battery-operated lights to spell out the name of the town so that a B-24, lost, low on fuel, and unable to receive radio transmissions could find its bearings and a safe landing place. It was imperative that they find a field where the heavy bomber could set down—and soon!

The plane circled our field for minutes while we trainees held our collective breath. Then apparently our fire signals got through, for the plane tipped its wing in a grateful salute and headed off in the direction of the nearest large base. We had all taken part in playing lighthouse for our fellow airmen in trouble, and we felt good about it. We hoped that someone might one day return the favor. Remembering that happy ending helped me understand my mother's actions in her fight against the darkness and her role in keeping the lights of home burning. It also helped me understand the role of millions of other mothers and the words of John Milton: "They also serve who only stand and wait."

Today's few active lighthouses have sophisticated electronic equipment, and so do the mariners on their ships. Lighthouses are not being built anymore, yet neither are they being torn down—except by time and the furious erosion of the sea. The ones in need of repair are being cared for, often by private citizens and their contributions and their visits to the sites. For what symbol of our past is more dramatically inspiring than those towers of light—from the Statue of Liberty to the smallest and most remote structure marking the entrance to a river or a harbor in Northern New York or Maine? What mission is more noble than saving lives and helping others in distress?

There are still those who remember being a part of a light-house keeper's family, for it was a lifestyle that involved the whole family. Today it involves only a routine check in spring and fall. Some remember it as a time of almost painful loneliness and boredom, with only the sound of the surf as background music. Some remember it as a time of trips to the mainland for school or shopping. Others remember listening to the mournful sound of the foghorns vibrate in the night and watching the buoys marking time on the place the sound seemed to have died. Some remember their lighthouse times with affection and gratitude for the family life and the closeness of family members, for the security of those walls, almost like a fortress against the outside world and the threatening sea.

During the summer I hope to make another pilgrimage to some of those towers of light, if only as a tourist. I would gladly become one of those lighthouse fanatics who, panting and sweating, climb the spiral staircase to a view overlooking water and those blood-red sunsets and drowning horizons. I would gladly wear my lighthouse T-shirt and carry the right maps and charts. I would gladly be a fool for *auld lang syne,* for a mother's devotion to the light, and for the sake of all those gallant ghosts lingering beyond the shoreline.

Look Homeward, Angel

"LOOK Homeward, Angel!" the poet implores in *Paradise Lost.* But where is home and how do we find it? Which home? Our childhood home? The home we made for our family? The home where we spent most of our lives? The home of our greatest happiness? And how do we know when we arrive there? For many the search for home is life-long, a journey not only in search of hearth but in search of Self.

For my maternal grandmother a house was not a home until someone had been born there, had lived there and died there, the life cycle in miniature. For her, a newborn had to sound its fragile protest and someone had to sigh a last breath. For her, those were the most authentic consecrations for a housewarming: the rites of home ownership demanded more than gifts, good wishes and champagne toasts; they demanded living, aging, sacrifice and devotion. And in a curious way my grandmother became her own benediction, for she died in our home, thereby gracing us with the last of her requirements for ownership, the leaving of it. Our mother made a long and lonely trip across a continent to bring her back, and although she was brought home to die, her parting gift was life in abundance for those who continued to live there.

For our mother, home was a place of light—a lighthouse in a sometimes cruel sea. A place where lights burned protectively at night. The window light; the guiding light. The reading light when sleep would not come. The worry light. The vigil light in the sick room. The night light that calmed a child's fears. And especially those lights from within, the love lights that burned with a familial constancy. And intensity.

For others there were definitions shaped by their separate experiences.

"Home is where the heart is."

"Home is journey's end."

"Any place I hang my hat is home."

"To Adam, Paradise was home. To the good among his descendants home is Paradise."

"Home is the place where, when you have to go there, they have to take you in."

"Be it ever so humble, there's no place like home."

And so it goes: words cynical, glib, sentimental, spiritual—all attempting to define this mysterious and magical place called *home.* So one begins to wonder if home is a place or a state of mind. One begins to wonder: is it made of brick, wood, adobe, mud—or memories?

I once read of a fashionable suburb in which there was no hospital and no cemetery. Its citizens joked, somewhat bitterly, that you couldn't be born there and you couldn't be interred there. And for some there was a strange and chilling feeling of affluent homelessness that prompted them to designate and record in their wills and last testaments the final permanent place. Perhaps some prairie town a thousand miles to the east or perhaps out behind some fenced-in plot on a Vermont farm. Some place where there are ties that bind, names, familiar and carved in stone. Sometimes in their 30's and 40's they made early plans for a final resting place, an eternity denied them in their fashionable precincts. Orphaned as they were by the gods of plenty, they still looked homeward.

I have read too of a place called *Miyajima,* near Hiroshima in Japan, seen pictures of this shrine island. It is a sacred place where no one is born and where no one dies. Mortality is a kind of desecration in this place where the spirits are said to dwell. It is a place of delicate grace and beauty where people go to meditate and heal.

I know of a another place that is *wakaN* or holy. It has been a part of my own life. It is a place that seems to be empty and desolate and forbidding. It is on a Lakota Native American reservation in South Dakota. To the people who live there it is full of the spirits of place, not far from the place they consider the center of the earth.

There is a tarpaper shack that sits forlornly on a prairie hilltop like a dark bird hatching loneliness. But the outside is deceiving: inside there are two generations living in harmony. Surrounding the cabin there are canvas tipis and several purification lodges that serve the *tiyospaye,* the extended family. The summer I was visiting, a *lila tate,* a July tornado blew their home apart like a bomb explosion. No one was home at the time: they were all at an Indian celebration in a nearby community.

When my friend told me of his plans to re-build on the same spot I questioned his decision. But he just gave me a ye-of-little-faith look and explained: "I dreamed it first and then I built it and now I will build it again. *WakaNtanka* (the Great Spirit) spared all of us. There is no need to leave our home."

A prairie kind of faith! *Home* is indeed made of such stuff!

And then there are the homes of memory, the homes gone but not forgotten.

Beginning in my mother's 97th year some homing instinct combined with memory prompted her to announce: "Well, I'd better be going home now." Her words usually came about four o'clock in the afternoon as she looked north, scanning the skies like an aviator about to take off. There was a look of shining anticipation as she spoke. On her lap was her only baggage for the trip, her "Book of Hope," a year-old telephone directory from her childhood home. Someone had sent for it to appease her in her search for familiar names and familiar places. But for her, now in a strange world, the passage of time had made no difference, for her home had not changed since World War I and she was a little girl again. It was the world that had changed!

"I'd better be going home now," she would repeat anxiously.

She never got there, of course, except in memory. Although her childhood home was only two hundred miles away I didn't take her back because I feared the harsher reality that waited for her. The disillusionment. Better let her have her bright vision, I decided. Better let home stay there in the corners of memory. Better let home be a place of childhood; a place to harvest dreams. The very old need so badly to go home again, to complete the great circle.

Anatomically, the womb was our first home and our mothers were the ones with whom we shared our first heartbeats. It was the place where all our needs were met; the place of sustenance. The place of safety and warmth. It was the earthly quintessential home, the paradise of flesh and blood. But it could not last: after a time we were expelled, drawn into a world not of our own making. Before we could walk or speak we became searchers after home once more.

According to Genesis our home was Eden: it was a part of the plan. A garden! A Paradise! A forever place! But forever proved to be bitterly brief and our garden turned to wasteland because of Adam's fall through pride and disobedience. And, because he was our ancestral father who failed, we were all denied eternal life in this earthly paradise. We were expelled again and had to find another home, a lesser home. Look homeward, angel! And the search went on!

And so somewhere between the longitude of longing and the latitude of loss we built our homes once again because we had to. We had to try to duplicate the home of the womb, the home of Eden. We had to try to find the place of belonging, the place of security, the place where the horizon no longer beckons. The place of emotional equilibrium. The kinder place. The place to spend the remaining time.

There is one more home, a waiting home, a permanent home that has been promised the believer. It lies on the other side: its foundation is hope and, when mixed with the mortar of faith, it will stand for eternity. It is the home celebrated in the Black spiritual that sings: "Home at last! Home at last! Thank God All-Mighty I'm home at last!"

Ultimately, home may be within us. I remember talking briefly with a homeless man on a mean city street. He was dragging a plastic bag full of his earthly belongings.

"That's not the only baggage I'm carrying," he told me.

I looked around but didn't see any other bags, shopping carts or old suitcases. He answered my puzzled stare by pointing to his head. "In here," he said. "Somewhere inside, there is the baggage of memory—that's where home really is."

He smiled when he said it, as though he had rounded a corner and there was a little cottage with a loving wife and child waiting for him. And then a shadow fell across his face and he became the loner and a searcher again. I wished him Godspeed and under my breath added: keep looking homeward, angel. Keep looking! All of us do!

A Surrogate Son

SHE was an old woman who was dying. Her eyes already had the gray and hooded look of a dead hawk and her voice was fragile as a fading echo. Yet, from somewhere deep inside, there was an indefinable spark that burned; she was somehow still on the side of life, only one foot in eternity.

I passed her room daily on my way to visit a friend in the Public Health Service Hospital in Rosebud, South Dakota on the Lakota (Sioux) Indian Reservation. As I went by her room she would frequently be singing in her native language, singing a nasal, sing-song chant that was almost a keening. The first day I heard her song I recognized it as a Death Song and sometimes I would pause outside her room long enough to get some of the words. After some eavesdropping I was able to piece it together.

Come, let me see it once more,
This land I love.
Only the hills last forever!

As a song of leaving it was a wonder, as pure an art form as could be imagined. Not art for art's sake but for *life's* sake. A song of ending at the very end; a song of departure. Her last words put to music. Hearing it again and again I shivered to think it was the final creation of an old woman, a summing up of all she knew or would say. Three lines! She wanted to see the land once more, the land she loved. Perhaps she wanted the blinds on the window drawn so that she could see the prairie waves roll in on a burnished tide. And then she put her philosophy in five words: "Only the hills last forever!" For her, that was all there was to say: all else was redundant.

Artistically it was perfect!

As I stood outside her door I accused myself of assorted betrayals—of eavesdropping, of intruding on a time that, for her, was *wakaN,* sacred or holy. I accused myself of insensitivity. Sometimes I felt like a person listening in on a private conversation or someone's confession to a priest. But the scholar and song collector in me was stronger than the moralist and I committed the song to memory where it still remains. I had come almost two thousand miles to collect and preserve the songs of the Lakota people and this was an opportunity not to be missed. I owed it to myself and to others to make my scholarship as accurate as possible. I was much younger then as well: today I might have deferred to age and privacy and to the memory of my own Death Song, to be sung when the time came, *my* time . . . Today I might have left her with her last words and her moments with *WakaNtaNka,* the Great Spirit. I might not have rushed in where angels fear to tread.

Thinking of the old woman's Death Song, I seemed to hear an echo in some lines by Christina Rosetti: "When I am dead, my dearest, sing no sad songs for me . . ." And it was so with the old woman. There was no self-pity in her song, no grief at leaving the only life she had known. There was just a celebration of life and her long stay on the earth. A celebration of the earth as well! This singing of a song of her own creation was, in a sense, her moment with God. And the brevity of her song amazed me as well. I remember later asking an informant why the personal songs of Native Americans were so brief. He smiled tolerantly. "They say it all," he told me. "The bottom line."

I couldn't argue with that.

A few days later, when I returned to see my friend, I discovered that he had left, just walked out against the doctor's advice. I knew he was tired of the sterility of the hospital, the dull routines, the long, lonely hours. Back in his own community illness was something of a social occasion. Family and friends gathered around; there was feasting, dancing, smoking the pipe. There was sympathy, companionship, conviviality—a kind of celebration almost. The hospital, in contrast was a white person's place, a place where the sick were isolated, left alone for hours at a time. My friend's leaving had taken away my reason for returning to the hospital but I showed up anyway.

I inquired about the old woman on the first floor, the one who kept singing her Death Song. What was wrong with her? How much time did she have left? Cancer, they told me. A few days now maybe.

I asked about her family, friends. I hadn't noticed any visitors.

They told me that only her son was left; the others had all passed away. They were trying to locate him. Then one of the doctors made a strange request. He asked me if I would stand in for the son, just be there, a physical presence in a darkened room. The old woman was nearly blind and she hadn't been with her son in years. Just sit there in the room, he asked. Just be there.

"What if she speaks to me?" I asked. "My Lakota isn't all that good, you know."

"She isn't really with it," another of the doctors said, touching his forehead. "She's in a faraway time, in a faraway place. The only things she says are the words to her song."

I felt that I owed the old woman something, some compassion, maybe even some companionship for stealing her song, her sharing with God. Maybe this would atone for what I was beginning to consider a wrong. Maybe it would set things right. I'm not sure exactly what I did think.

Anyway I agreed to do it.

For those last five days I watched and waited and listened to her unwavering song of praise and courage. I liked to think what I was doing was for my own mother as well, that I was a son straddling two cultures, that I had been adopted by both women, by time and absence.

On that last day at a few minutes after ten in the morning the old woman died with her song on her lips. She was singing and suddenly there was a sound like berry boxes breaking and then a silence that told me it was over. I was at the window when she died, opening the blinds. When she had sung the words, "Come, let me see it once more . . ." I had risen from my chair and gone to the window, as though in response to her words, as though on cue.

A few days later I went to the funeral at the Catholic mission. There were eight people there. I learned that the old woman had returned to the reservation from Chicago where she had spent most of her life. She had no identification, nothing but a Catholic medal around her neck that the nurses had discovered. There was also a brief, year-old letter in her pocket, a letter from a son in California. That was all. It was almost as though she had shown up just to die. The padre had tried to contact her son in Los Angeles but had failed. The padre had heard that I was with her for a few days at the end, that I had known her. I told him no, I was just standing in for her son; I was just someone in the room—a warm, breathing body; a hand to reach out to. A stranger. He asked me if there were any words I could say. I said she had said it all herself in her Death Song.

There was nothing else for me to add.

The priest said a few words about the old woman. The circle is a sacred symbol for the Lakota. She had perhaps come full circle, back to the beginning again.

That was all there was. An old Lakota woman had shown up to die. She belonged because she was a Lakota and where there were accepting Lakota hearts, anyone belonged; there was the *tiyospaye*, the extended family group, the community, that gave her welcome, even as she was leaving.

Thirty years have passed now and the old woman, for me, has *become* her song. I no longer see her, even through the eye of memory, but, if the wind is westerly I can hear her still. I hear her song of thanksgiving, her song of praise. I hear her sing of the things that endure, even prevail. I hear her sing a Death Song whose meaning is life, a song beyond language, culture and race—fragile as age, yet strong as hope.

Part Three

The Long Good-bye

Lost and the Miracle of Being Found

A LONG time ago, a little boy approached me on a street in my hometown and told me that he was lost. I asked him if he knew his address. He nodded and dutifully recited it, an address, strangely, only a few blocks away. I told him I knew where it was and would take him home, but he shook his head.

"I know my way home," he said, now on the verge of tears.

"Then you aren't lost," I told him.

"Yes," he insisted, "I'm lost *inside.*" He said it desperately, pathetically, like a stranger in a strange land to an inept and insensitive translator. "You know . . . heart-lost."

At the time I didn't know what he meant. I didn't know his past. I didn't know his troubles, anxieties, and traumas. And perhaps I didn't care as much as I should have. To me he was just a little boy lost in some way or other—perhaps only in his imagination. Not knowing what else to do, I took him home and left him on his front porch. I had a nagging feeling that I had failed him in some important way, perhaps had even betrayed him. But I could not stay; I was young and my own life was waiting.

I am much older now, and that brief encounter has grown more meaningful with each passing year. *Lost inside!* A geography more tortuous and compelling than the streets of any town. And with no possible map! None at all!

Over the years I have become acquainted with the lost. I have studied them, written about them, even loved them. At times I have been one of them. But that little boy lost was the one who first prompted me to ask myself, *What does it really mean to be lost, to be unable to find my way back to where I came from or want to be?* It was a question that was to haunt me, a question another would ask me tearfully one sad and distant day. She would be in her hundredth year—the mother to whom I was devoted and whose memory lives on in me still.

Lost . . .

. . . strayed, misplaced, or missing. I lost my dog . . . my keys . . . my wallet. Things I once had are now gone. But those are little things in the grand scheme. What about issues more significant, more vital? What about things like belief, faith? "I have lost my faith" means so much more. Such a loss has greater consequences, more like worlds falling. In such a context the meaning of the word *lost* swells like a river at flood time and becomes just as dangerous.

. . . to go astray, especially morally: a lost person. To lose one's moral compass, one's direction. Some would say to lose one's soul. Great literature is replete with examples—Dr. Faustus, Captain Ahab, Macbeth—all lost! All barter their souls for something temporal, some perceived earthly treasure that "moth and rust doth corrupt"—power, fame, adulation, domination, pleasure, wealth, or vengeance. And in the unwise barter, each becomes the thing he most despises.

We find them in history as well, those who have sold out to their appetites, their obsessions, their consuming ambitions. They are no less tragic figures; whatever other sins or crimes they committed, the greatest were betrayal of God and of self. All lost!

Lost . . .

. . . no longer practiced, a *lost* art. I remember an old, dignified gentleman with a drooping, turned-down mustache who sat at a desk in the shade of a big city building. From that sheltered spot he practiced the lost art of fine handwriting, calligraphy. I remember stopping and watching him for minutes at a time as his hand swept the letters into being with an artistry I thought magical. Calling cards, notes, invitations—he would write anything with a flourish that sometimes stopped pedestrian traffic.

I remember too another old man, an organ grinder, who ground out the classical songs of Italy and the popular tunes of America while a rheumy, sad-eyed monkey performed antics for the crowd and then passed a tin cup for donations.

There are others, struggling or drowned in the swift currents of time: the shoe-shine boy, the iceman, the itinerant scissors sharpener, the gaudy dancers, minstrels and street performers, barnstormers, and the rest. The thoughtful letter writers and those who believe that good conversation is an art. All practitioners of a lost or dying art, all waiting in a high-tech present to become part of a remembered past.

Lost . . .

. . . bewildered, helpless, unable to cope or function—the way most of us are lost at times, especially toward the end of our lives when we are on borrowed time. Or when some dementia strikes and we are no longer what we once were. I shall always remember my mother's words, spoken in a rare moment of insight: "I have lost myself." And she spent so many hours of what turned out to be her last few years of life searching for that lost self.

That other self—victim of dementia, illness, frailty, and all those lesser afflictions—was the one with whom she had to grow old, her companion for a shorter journey, a long night's journey into light. Yet yesterday's child was still in there somewhere—child, daughter, wife, mother, teacher, and great soul. They would be survivors long after the wheelchair had turned to rust. She was lost then during the long dying, but we both prayed for the day when she would be found.

If being lost is one of the cruelest of emotional states, then its opposite, to be *found,* is the epitome of deliverance. To find oneself again! Not as one would stumble on something by accident in the dark of night but as one might discover a continent, a world, a comet, a faith. After planning, travel, study, danger and pain, and finally, enlightenment, it must be such a discovery—one that registers at least a seven on the soul's seismograph.

That lost boy so long ago—I let him down badly. He was telling me something important, a truth of the heart. He spoke as a child, and it was I who still saw through the glass darkly. He spoke of something I could not or would not see. "Heart-lost" he had said in his search for the right words, *lost inside!* And it had taken me nearly a lifetime to understand what he had meant.

Sometimes I cannot help but look at a newspaper's Lost and Found column; my eye is drawn to it as iron by a magnet. And sometimes I think I see "Lost in midtown Manhattan: homeless man; answers to 'Dad, Dear.' If found, please return to Fairhaven, N.Y. Eternal reward. " But usually there are no such surprises—there are only dogs strayed, wallets lost, wrist watches and keys missing. Sometimes things more personal: I.D. papers, checkbooks, credit cards . . . and wedding bands. But most of these items are only an honest heart and a phone call away from being found. In many cases a reunion of loser and lost item awaits, a meeting between finder and loser. Sometimes a monetary reward for the finder, sometimes just a heartfelt thanks . . .

Yet often I get the strange feeling that I am looking for more than just a brief and happy ending, for over the years I have built up a heavy burden of expectation. I believe I am looking for an epiphany, a discovery, even a revelation of sorts, something that will shake me up and change my angle of perception. Something that will challenge and perhaps change me in some important way, make me a better person. And perhaps this enlightenment will come to me in the guise of something or someone else—a miracle disguised in the ordinary. Perhaps I am looking for the truth of discovery, the miracle of being found but expressed in a different way—in the sad and paradoxical words of an old lady who meant the world to me. Or in the halting words of a little boy lost.

Among a Mother's Legacy

IN her final years, when my mother had returned to the past, to a time when her world was young and beautiful and full of loved ones, she usually carried with her a 50-year-old telephone directory which she called among other things her "Handbook of Memories." Slim and without advertising, it was also dog-eared and stuffed with handwritten notes, cards and newspaper clippings. It listed the names, addresses and four-digit numbers of a town as it once was but would never be again, the Town of Bethlehem in Albany County in Upstate New York. It was a directory of the past yet it chronicled her present reality, a reality that had never changed since our family settled there in the 1920's and, for her, a lover of literature, that treasured and much-used phone book had all the beauty and permanence of the written word.

Mother was approaching 100 at the time but the names of those in her book were forever outside time, frozen in print and the richer, more comforting dimension of always. And she would explain to her son that the names, addresses and numbers alone told an incomplete story. "The whole truth of things is always in the details," she would go on to say: "And living is our heartfelt expression of those details."

For a woman in the grip of some dementia her words were almost a truth inspired.

She had told me those things before and once again the past intruded on the present to shape a memory. We were visiting a friend's grave in a local cemetery. I was just a boy but it bothered me, almost to tears, that the carvings on the gravestones were so brief and stark—usually a name and two dates and sometimes a few words, a quotation perhaps to bridge the absence. To a boy knee-deep in the moment it seemed to be such a cruel shorthand for a life. After telling her my feelings I asked her about those words and their bitter brevity.

"We who loved them have to fill in the details," she would tell me as she stooped to plant a flower. "The details of their lives, that's our job to remember. Each time we remember we resurrect them so they're not just a name over two dates. It's like we wrote their heart's biography and carved it there in stone. It's all in the details; everything is in the details."

"Even God?" I asked, uncertain of what I meant yet wanting to include everything in my question.

"Even God," she answered. And then she added: "*Especially* God."

I didn't follow it up at the time. I didn't ask how God was in the details. I didn't ask what she meant. I was a boy and so there was always a "later on" to pursue the unfinished business of life. *God was in the details!* So I did the next best thing at the time: I remembered her words.

Now, whenever I visit a special cemetery the truth of her words comes back with an even greater impact for my own name and date of birth are now engraved beside hers in the finality of cold marble. And, after my name and date of birth is a space, a waiting and anticipatory space, wide as the distance between the poles it seems and loud as the silence between thunder claps. A long distance, a loud silence waiting to be filled. And sometimes that boyhood feeling returns and I find myself asking once again: Is this all? A name and two dates? And what of the heart's biography and those defining details that flesh out the person we once were? Those details my mother talked so much about?

I remember the terrible frustrations of a high school friend whose brother was killed in World War II. My friend and his parents tried to re-construct the dead airman's army service and last days and, of course, his death. Eventually, years later, their yearning for details led them across an ocean to stand before one certain grave in a stunted forest of white marble, there to read the words that confirmed the heart's longing and the shock of that War Department telegram that had begun: "The War Department regrets to inform you that your son . . ." And then, weeks later, a letter had come, a letter from another member of the flight crew, the only survivor of the wounded bomber, a letter full of details of that last mission and the courage and sacrifice of their son and brother, the co-pilot of the plane. The letter was written from a Stalag in Germany and it gave a family the particulars of the life and death of a young flier. It was not written in the telegraph-ese of a wartime bureaucracy but in the stumbling and awkward phrasing of a friend. It was the heart's details. It was not as dramatic as the white, marble cross, one among thousands in that manicured field. But the letter provided the details, the foundation for memories. It had done for the imagination what the cross had done for sight: it had provided a focus for the wounded heart.

Now there is a second and a third generation collecting mementoes and details of an airman lost in war. Now there are articles, pictures and medals, the details of his sacrifice. There are the wooden soldiers and model airplanes of a hero's boyhood. There are war stories ripe for telling. *It's all in the details!* For the airman's life was in the details! And it would have been a sin to make abstract what was flesh and blood and memories! The particulars are necessary to put a life together again. Lest we forget!

Later, when I became a writer, I drew on my mother's words of wisdom again as I constructed details for imaginary characters, trying to make them come alive for my readers. And, with almost every sentence I wrote I could feel her looking over my shoulder and whispering ". . . everything is in the details."

And so I asked once more: "Even God?" And this time I thought I knew the answer to that question. For the God I believed in, that we both believed in, had shared our humanity: in the vernacular of the street He had not only talked the talk, but He had walked the walk. And He had left us the details of that all-important sharing in words, rituals, miracles, sacraments, institutions and example. He had left his footprints, His fingerprints and His heart prints behind. He had given us the beginnings in Bethlehem and the Stations of His Leaving. He left us a vision to emulate, a vision of those ". . . better angels of our nature."

And, not the least of His legacies, He left us mothers to explain—and perhaps to justify.

The Refrigerator Anthology

EVEN as a boy I searched the refrigerator door for messages before I looked inside for food. Later I called the refrigerator an "anthology" for it was papered, almost to the point of insulation, by clippings—aphorisms, prayers, birth announcements, obituaries, literary quotations, poems and the primitive and creative efforts of several generations. Our family did not live by bread alone but by the written word as well. Some writings were even in Latin, some in French, which gave them an intriguing and classical spin. Others were popular and contemporary, the enduring and the ephemeral, an eclectic assortment. There were pictures too, mostly by my sister and me, drawn and colored for special occasions and holidays.

At first the refrigerator door and one exposed side served as the family's bulletin board of reminders and remainders. *Today is a holy day!* Next to a recipe for maple sugar cookies. *Bring home your report card!* Followed by a partial store list. Most of the announcements and reminders were changed or updated every few days but there were those marked "Save!" and they owed their permanence to words of beauty, significance or relevance: quotations, prayers, the words that made a connection, even though they hurt. *Mama has taken a turn for the worst.* These endured; turned yellow and brittle and were Scotch-taped over and over until almost obscured or else they were pieced together again like a fragile puzzle or until they were copied by a loving hand or typed and displayed again, a paper resurrection.

In its own way the refrigerator door told a history of our family, its activities, relationships and values. The dramatic and the mundane were represented; the sacred and the profane. The humorous and the tragic. It was our journal, our photo album, our memory bank. Over the years it expressed our hopes, our aspirations. And it also reflected change and the passing years.

If the refrigerator door was our anthology then mother was its editor-in-chief. Usually the extent of our father's involvement was taping a joke or a tennis schedule on any space where white showed through. And, under mother's editorship there was seldom an organizing principle. It was as though a dust devil had spun through the kitchen and plastered the refrigerator with what it spun from its vortex. Nor did mother show any prejudice toward what was included as long as it was ". . . in good taste," the only criterion for her censorship. And when the refrigerator ran out of space she would hang clippings over clippings, picture over picture, so many they had a skirted appearance and even rustled when the refrigerator door was opened.

Those were the days before refrigerator magnets with their cute, plastic sayings attached. *Money talks: mine says good-bye.* Or *Families are like fudge—mostly sweet with a few nuts.* And there were those that recalled the places you had visited or what baseball or football team you followed. There were the sayings that expressed a brief and simplistic philosophy or attitude in the way of bumper stickers and T-shirts. *No pain, no gain.*

During World War II there were pictures of men and women in uniform and what they had done and were doing and where they were. They had won their wings or the Silver Star, the Purple Heart or had graduated from Officer Candidates School. They had shipped out to unknown destinations. They had been promoted. And they had been lost— killed in action; missing in action; prisoners of war. They were ghost faces from faraway places on a refrigerator they might never again open for a Coke or a beer. Yet there were happy endings too—the return of heroes who came back to pick up the pieces of broken or interrupted lives, candidates for the Anthology once more.

Changes in the Refrigerator Anthology were gradual, but certain and discernible as aging itself. The influences of youth were far less visible. In the new and uncertain world we had become prisoners of hope and yet there were recurring whispers of sadness too as we all grew older.

> *We are such stuff*
> *As dreams are made on,*
> *And our little life*
> *Is rounded with a sleep . . .*

And: *Let me be strong enough to be glad of remembrance, rather than unkind in loss.*

As mother grew old and dad was gone and we children had moved away, I noticed on my visits that the grandchildren and then the great-grandchildren were represented in the Anthology. *Children are the living messages we send to a time we will not see.* There was a sadness in leaving also that had crept into the writings. *To know how to grow old is the masterwork of wisdom, and one of the most difficult chapters in the great art of living.* And: *Dear God, help me to grow old gracefully and without bitterness.* It was mother's greatest fear: this making an ungracious exit from life; the fear of being "twice a child," of becoming something she was not.

As mother reached her 80s her leaving became almost an obsession. She was like a great actress making her final exit in the last performance of a long career. She feared that she would be a burden to her children or that, in some way, she might betray the strong, intelligent, caring woman she had always been. That she might not retain her Self and her dignity to the end. She didn't fear death but she feared incapacity; she feared becoming something she was not. And so, prayers and secular sayings began to appear, not only in the Anthology, but on separate handwritten scraps of paper hidden in books and envelopes, scraps for God to find and heed, if He would.

In her early nineties her mind, guided by imagination, began a journey back to a happier time, the time of her childhood and youth. It is a time to which many of us return when the present seems too heavy to bear. It is both a defeat and a victory for one in life's inevitable autumn. It is a disease and a cure. For who among us does not spend a part of his or her time in memory's velvet grip? The past is all we really possess—the future is beyond us and the present rolls like mercury in our hands.

One dreary winter's day after mother's passing I returned to the house to begin the sad and difficult task of sorting through a lifetime. And finally I came to the Refrigerator Anthology, still festooned with its mix of trivia, wisdom and memories. I began to go through the paper past, large envelope in hand, picking what I wanted to preserve from the machine. And suddenly I came across a brief message, written in her own unsteady hand and dated several months before her death. I stooped to read it and the words went through me like a blade: *I shall not call you back. And I shall rejoice!* As clear and poignant as anything she had ever written! And next to it, the last piece of paper left on the refrigerator, a quote from Saint Exupery, French author and aviator, killed in World War II: *If you love something . . . set it free!*

And, as the years passed, I have set many things free, things I loved and lost to the world or time. I have set free all but the memories.

If you love something . . . set it free!

Those are good words for an ending and I shall always remember them as my mother did. I plucked the remaining words from the refrigerator lovingly, as a farmer might pick the last of his bountiful harvest. And for the first time in sixty years the Refrigerator Anthology, which fed us body and soul, stood pale and naked in the failing light.

From Mourning into Morning

I STILL think of the experience as one of my stations along the way, although I didn't realize its importance at the time. To really understand, you have to look backward; you need the advantages of both perspective and hindsight. But life doesn't wait for analysis, and we have to live it forward, a moment at a time. And so all those little revelations go by almost without recognition. That is how it was with this station.

I had arrived early for Mass, travel weary and in a strange town. I sat up front in the empty church, under a statue of Saint Joseph, who was holding a T-square in one hand and the Christ Child in the other, as though balancing love and duty. Shadows projected by the flames of votive candles in a nearby rack danced on the wall beside him. The effects were hypnotic. My eyes went from shadow to flame and back to shadow, and I watched and listened as one candle died a sputtering and trembling death. A few moments later a thin column of smoke rose in the calm like a signal to mark the place. And I thought, somewhat sadly, *another memory extinguished. A memory become a memory . . .*

Suddenly, and for no apparent reason, I found myself rising from my pew and going to the candle rack, where I knelt on a padded bench. Then, taking a taper from a special partition in the rack, I stole a living flame from a dying one and lighted a fresh candle. The flame blossomed instantly and became a living thing: life from death, a resurrection fire.

I knew at once that on some level it was all a memorial to my mother, who had died three months before in the dead of winter. For with the lighting of the candle, there was also a blooming in my heart—a prayer so fervent that it would not be shaped by words but only by fire.

I watched the memorial flame for what could have been minutes or hours as it performed a dance of death on its own melting. Then suddenly the flame began to dance more wildly—like a jealous and vengeful Salome, with the music faster. I felt a breeze and turned to see an old woman enter the church through a side door. The spell was broken: things became again what they seemed. I rose and returned to my seat.

It was nothing really, a moment's trance, a traveler's escape from the road. The lighting of a candle. A love gone and the pain of absence. A prayer-flame. A forged memory. A blessed intrusion on the moment. It was nothing—and yet everything! One of those rare moments in which mystery burns for a while and the inexplicable happens and time hangs suspended. A moment that just is— beyond all design, expectation, and certainly, analysis.

All during the Mass I found myself distracted, staring at the open flames that moved in unison to the whirring overhead fans, like pale dancers in a chorus line. And as I watched, I wondered, *How many candles had burned for me over the years? How many had been lighted by my mother and grandmother during the war years with but a single intention—to bring me back safely to home and parish? How many petitions, stations, and rosaries had been mumbled over those spitting candles that would not last the week?*

I looked at the altar candle that I had been told would burn always as a visible sign of God's presence there. My grandmother had told me that when I was just a boy, and I remember being greatly impressed. *Always* seemed like such reassurance against the doubts, dangers, and changes of the world. It was like an anchor dropped deep in angry waters.

My grandmother also told me a story that my father had told her. During the first World War a church had been destroyed in a French village, all but the altar candle, which had miraculously survived an enemy shelling. And there it was in the rubble, a pulse of flame that kept beating from the moment's ruin. The story became one of those truths of the heart that I have carried with me over the years—a parable according to Mama.

Another thought followed like a wave upon a wave: I had never before lighted a holy candle in church—not for an intention, not for myself, not for another. And, God knows, I had reason enough to signal for help over the years. But I couldn't—or wouldn't—make the connection between a naked flame and a Lord's possible intervention. For in those days I was still caught up in my newly discovered rationality, and the only lights I recognized were those of reason and logic. Now I know better.

I had, however, lighted holy candles at home many times during the thunder and lightning storms that so frightened my mother. But her fear remained, and the candles continued to burn. When the storms finally passed, the candles might be extinguished, but they were never put away until winter's enforced armistice.

As a lifelong Catholic I knew the symbolic value of candles and their long history in church ritual and ceremony. I had long witnessed the lighting of candles before Mass. I had seen the blessing of candles on Candlemas and the candles lighted for All Souls' Day. I had prayed before a lighted candle on top of a coffin. I had marched in processions carrying a flame. Light and life and memory, those flames seemed to symbolize to me: the lighted path, the breath of life, the way through the dark of forgetfulness. I had known them all.

In the secular world, too, I had blown out birthday candles, had melted candles down into other candles. I had seen candles burning beside some roadside memorial. I had carried emergency candles in the trunk of my car. I had even set up candles as death traps for moths that couldn't help themselves in this last game they played. And hadn't I, too, been drawn to the flame that strange Sunday morning when my mother's death so filled my heart and mind? It was a kind of delayed reaction to my mother's leaving, a ritual that somehow required a period of gestation. Or perhaps it was the opposite: a spontaneous memorial that needed only a spark. I couldn't be sure. Yet I had felt as though something or someone of the spirit had touched me on the shoulder and whispered ever so softly: "Now! It is time." And I had risen and followed where the spirit led.

Whether a candle flame or a conflagration, fire captures the attention and the imagination. Whether a mythical bird rises from its ashes to a new beginning or a martyred saint rises to glory through it, fire is one of the great symbolic creator-destroyers. Whether a candle of remembrance, a candle of protection, a candle of blessing, a candle of heraldry, a candle of signaling, or a candle of illumination—each is part of a long tradition. Thus far science has given us nothing to replace that small bud of flame.

My own epiphany (for that was what it was) came from a spiritual awakening that morning: from my self-discoveries, from my own reunion with myself and the past. It happened in a strange place but in a familiar church, a place different yet the same. And it wasn't *what* happened so much as the *way* it happened—all beyond and outside me, as though I were a compass needle spinning ever north.

Looking back on the brief and private ceremony, I can better understand my discoveries, even though knowledge came late and slowly, like a truth's dawning. I discovered that memory can be active in our lives, that it can choose us as well as be chosen, almost in an echo of the Lord's gentle rebuke in John 15: "You did not choose me. I chose you."

I discovered too that after memory has claimed us, it may also charge us with certain responsibilities—not only to

remember but also to include the departed in our living, perhaps in the way that many Mexican people include their
ancestors in their activities on the Day of the Dead, a colorful
holiday of the spirits' return that complements what we
know as All Souls' Day. For by coming to terms with the
dead and the part they still play in our lives, we acknowledge the probability of angels among us. We recognize the
visitation in a candle flame. We testify to the miracle of the
Resurrection. Then the moment's grief becomes something
else, something more healing and closer to victory as we
move from mourning into morning.

Double Exposures

AFTER my parents died and our childhood home was sold because both my sister and I had established independent lives elsewhere I decided to take one last photograph for *auld lang syne's* sake. I knew the place might not ever again look the same. There was a woods on one side of our home, a woods that, I feared, could all too easily be converted into a building lot in this very desirable neighborhood location. There were birches and maples we had planted in the front yard over the years, some bearing the carved names of old girlfriends and crude engravings of hearts with arrows through them, the woundings of young love. There were several with the initials of the dead, classmates who had died too early and deserved a special constancy of remembrance—a cross or a flower. My mother's flowers lined the paved driveway, the perennials—tulips, daffodils, crocuses, jonquils and hyacinths that celebrated their own rising on bursts of color. There were the rose bushes that climbed the white picket fence of our neighbor. And in the back yard there were colored stones marking the burial places of a boy's treasures and a robin's demise. And, of course, the thousand memories of the past.

I decided to take a view from the front, focused and snapped the shutter—a sound foreboding, louder than expected, a sound that seemed to mark the end of something, as though I had fired a shot into my past. Yet I thought that some day I might return and, with the new owner's permission, take another photograph, a sort of before-and-after comparison of time and memory.

A few weeks later I took a picture of my new living quarters on the same roll of film, but through some mistake or malfunction the film failed to advance. When I examined the prints I discovered a double exposure, a house superimposed on a home. It was an unintentional portrait of the persistence of memory, of the past haunting and even illuminating the present. In some ways it was a disturbing and ghostly picture. At first it reminded me of a face seen in the ruins or a face under water and then it reminded me of those childhood games where you look for faces in a natural scene. You had to tip and turn the picture or your head at different angles in order to see the faces hidden in trees and clouds and streams. Yet, for some reason I did not discard my double exposure: I put it away in a desk drawer without knowing exactly why.

Months later on a return visit to my former hometown I planned to take another picture, this time a deliberate double exposure for artistic effect but when I arrived, my home, as I had known it, was gone! The woods next door had disappeared and the partial skeleton of a new house was rising like a ghostly intruder. The maples and birches we had planted so lovingly and so long ago were gone! Most of my mother's flowers that bordered the driveway were gone and so too was the dogwood tree in the back yard and even the rose bushes! It was as though Memory's cruel harvest had come to take it all away, separating the past from the present.

I had informed the owners I was coming and they happened to be going away for the day so I had the place to myself. For minutes I just stood there, camera in hand, looking at the two homes, the one in my memory and the one physically before me now, the two superimposed again somewhere inside my head—or my heart. Suddenly I felt a chill of absence and of loss too and I knew I would never return to this endearing place again, that my reasons for doing so were gone. The place, the people—there was a difference never to be overcome! And standing there in the middle of spring I felt a winter in my heart. Slowly I put my camera back in its case and moved on. I did not look back.

Nor have I returned home, so cruelly transformed. Over the years I have returned to my hometown many times to visit relatives, friends and the fields where they rest, but I have never gone *home* again, except in my imagination.

The print of my double exposure was lost in one of my moves, but I do not regret the loss because its negative has been impressed on my heart, the dark area made lighter by remembrance. The picture still invites questions, important questions I still reflect on. In the intervening years I have come to think of life itself as a double exposure with the past, which never really dies, breaking through to illuminate the present. I have also tried to define, if only to myself, the difference between a house and a *home*. Poets have tried with varying degrees of success. One calls it ". . . where the heart is." And that is good. Another calls it ". . . the place we start from." And that is good also. But I shall always think of *home* as a double exposure, with the past bursting through like the sun from behind a cloud.

Sometimes, in my more nostalgic moments I think of going back, driving down that once-familiar street and stopping in front of the house that was once *home*. Sometimes in the minutes between sleep and wakefulness the reunion of heart and hearth all plays out in my mind. I see things as I used to see them, with eyes still young. I feel things as I used to feel them, with nerves sensitive as harp strings. But the trouble is that I see things as *they* are and not as I am. I see a select piece of real estate that is not *real* and certainly far from an *estate*. I am a stranger seeing a stranger's place and through a stranger's eyes.

Saying good-bye is always difficult. So is letting go. Yet we are reminded constantly that ". . . to everything there is a season." A season for parting; a season for letting go as well. But the memories, those double exposures of the heart are always there just beneath the surface, layered and waiting and inviting all those precious times to be lived over again in the welcome tranquility of a new moment.

Mother's Shooting Star

ON the night of my mother's death, I watched a shooting star blaze across the sky from east to west. My first impulse was to fall on my knees in awe. But there were people around.

When I had seen the star, I had felt a vital connection between my mother's passing and the meteor's fall from the heavens. It was as though an indifferent world had spared a few seconds to signal that one of its daughters—and a great soul—had left this life for eternity. A sign. A first bud of healing. After nearly a century, she had given up the ghost and was out there somewhere on the soul's solitary orbit, fueled by a lifetime of love, faith, hope, and prayers.

A day or so after her death, her cold and factual obituary leaped out at me from among 22 others. But there was no mention of a shooting star.

Yet the choice was still mine: epiphany, revelation, or indifferent coincidence? The world's truth or the truth of the heart? I had the feeling I was too close to it, my grief too recent, to decide. And I wondered at that. Most of her years had been good ones. I had not expected her to live forever. But she had been a part of my life for so long, I could not imagine a world without her.

What I needed was perspective on the matter, a perspective that was sympathetic to the spiritual.

Naturally, I thought of Ruben. He was an old friend who had helped me gather the songs and legends of his people, the Lakota. He lived in a prairie shack that had no running water or electricity. With no more than a fourth-grade education, he nevertheless possessed an intuitive, native folk wisdom. To his people, Ruben was a *wicasa wakaN*, a holy man. I remember he used to tell me there were two ways of looking at life: as though *nothing* was a mystery or as though *everything* was a mystery. I needed to hear what he would say about the juxtaposition of the shooting star and my mother's death.

And so I wrote him in care of his tiny community, hoping it was enough of an address. I enclosed a stamped, self-addressed envelope and hoped for the best. Ruben's tradition was oral. I didn't even know if he could write.

But two weeks later I received a reply: *Mikola (my friend): I am glad you still pay attention to things* wakaN, *(sacred, holy). All things are joined. Nothing is separate. In this world or the Other. For some special souls, a star can light the way. You know your mother best. Is she such a special one?*

I thought long and hard about his question before I answered.

Yes, Ruben. She *is* special enough for that celestial escort!

It was like a sunburst on a cloudy, day. And in that magic moment, I no longer saw through a glass darkly but face to face.

My original impulse had been to fall on my knees, to acknowledge the mystery I had witnessed even though I did not understand. Thinking too much can sometimes cloud an issue, make one impotent in thought or action. Consequently, all the things I had counted on for support—my experience, education, background—had betrayed me.

I went to my mother's notebook of quotations and fragments that she had copied over the years. After thumbing through its pages for an hour or so, I came across this quote from Greek author Nikos Kazantzakis: "The highest point a person can attain is not knowledge, or virtue, or goodness, or victory, but something even greater, more heroic . . . sacred awe!"

Inwardly, I smiled for the first time in a long while: my mother was still teaching me.

But even several months after the sighting of the meteor, I remained troubled by my failure to react to the drama played out in the sky. I had experienced "sacred awe." And while I might have acknowledged it by bowing down— or at least genuflecting—I had been influenced by cynicism and doubt.

Maybe someday I will make another choice, for God is generous with second chances. It may be a comet or a meteor. Or it may be something as mundane as my mother's perennials poking through winter's crust along the edges of her driveway.

It has been seven years now since my mother's passing, and already I have developed an affinity for stars and the galaxies beyond. Her shooting star has drawn me there just as memory's gravity has held me here.

I have also taken great comfort in her book of hope. I read it often and have noticed that stars play a part in her geography of hope. Consider this line, one she wrote in 1990: "Are the stars so brightly lit to help each one of us find his way across?"

I suspect by now she knows the answer.

A Lifetime of Words,
An Eternity of Silence

EACH time I visit my parents' graves in upstate New York, I take with me a black wooden bead from a broken rosary. I do not know how the beads came to be broken, but they belonged to my mother, and to her mother before her. I found them in an envelope tucked away in a dresser drawer after my mother's death. In a ritual I follow strictly but do not understand, I poke a hole in the ground next to the brown granite marker, bury the single bead, and cover up the hole. I find that I can do it even in wintertime, when snow is on the ground.

There is more hope than despair in the ritual, although at times the bead reminds me of a dark tear falling. It is a burial of sorts, but a burial of hope and expectation, like planting a seed in springtime. And it is my way of letting them know I was there, a sign, if you will, of their continued presence among the living as well as a record of my visit. It is a bit like leaving a note in the milk box when I was a boy.

I do not know whether the beads I plant will eventually go downward to where my parents lie or rise to the surface again. A Lakota friend once told me that beads lying on the ground often indicate the location of a Native American grave. It seems that beads, buried with the body, are carried to the surface by ants and other insects. He said that was how anthropologists and grave robbers locate the burial sites. I wonder whether the beads I bury will go down under the weight of sorrow or autumn rains and winter snows. Though I am not sure, I feel that they might eventually ascend to blossom in a burst of glory.

During those graveside visits I pray for my parents and talk to them, especially my mother. In life she and I had a

wonderfully verbal relationship, spending long hours talking about everything from literature and philosophy to eternity. She did not play with my sister and me; she was not a
physical person. My father was the one to join in and even
create the fun and games we enjoyed during childhood and
in later life. But our mother played on language as on an
organ. A former Latin teacher, she could, even in old age,
speak a stately, formal Latin that always reminded me of
Caesar's legions marching.

Her English, too, ran lyric and pure. She read to me, and
the words have stayed with me for a lifetime. She started
with *A Child's Garden of Verses* by Robert Louis Stevenson,
almost her contemporary. She bought books for me. She tested me. She did what all my early teachers could not do—she
instilled in me a love of the spoken and written word that
survived even the rebellion and defiance of my teenage
years. More than anyone else, she gave my life a purpose and
a direction, even without my cooperation.

Later, after I'd graduated from high school, she fought
more than one guidance counselor for what she thought was
my rightful place in a college, and during World War II she
wrote me heart-deep letters that told me what the war was
all about from a civilian mother's moral and philosophical
perspective. She took away the GI doubts and the narrow
vision that a soldier usually has. She was my benefactor, my
cheerleader, and my advocate. She kept my connection to
home a live one. And I felt the quiet power of her prayers as
surely as I felt the weight of stars and the whisper of winds.

She was a spiritual mentor to my sister and me as well. My
father was a good and sensitive man, but his Presbyterian
faith had been diluted by what he perceived as the injustices
and unfairness of the world. Though he was a social, fun-
loving man, the comfort of religion somehow did not cancel
out the pain that life surprised him with from time to time.

Never once, though, did he interfere with my mother's determination to raise us in the Catholic faith. He even encouraged us to live according to our adopted beliefs and to be good at whatever we did—at athletics, as Scouts, or at being good Catholics. More introspective and philosophical, our mother was the one who dealt with the big questions while our father tried his best to protect us from the slings and arrows of a world's singular meanness or indifference.

The silence of dead mothers! I remember a friend from grade school, along with his mother. He was a sickly, frail child, and I recall how his mother would walk several miles on rainy days to bring his rubbers or overshoes or a thermos of hot soup or his latest medication. The other children made fun of both of them, of course. But when the teasing turned to bullying, I became his friend and protector, a role that continued on into high school.

At our fiftieth high school reunion, I discovered that my friend had been drafted in World War II and was killed in the Battle of the Bulge. My informant was a mutual friend who had been in his outfit and was with him at the end. He told me that in those hectic and panicky days of the German breakthrough, my boyhood friend had been forced to stay behind in a foxhole because his feet were frozen and he could neither advance nor retreat. When the enemy overwhelmed his position, he had been killed.

Even over drinks with old friends, I was suddenly struck by the irony of those events as they were described to me. Somehow, in some crazy way, I would have expected his protective mother to show up with his rubbers or overshoes once more and save him as he crouched in his foxhole and awaited the end. This would have been the ultimate in dramatic and happy endings, but my faith had taught me to believe in miracles. Also, I know that a mother's love is a force as powerful as any on earth.

I remember a time when my own mother called a high-ranking officer in the Air Force when she had not heard from me in what she thought was a long time. I discovered this at another reunion at which I met the officer in question, a man who turned out to be a general. As we shook hands I half-apologized for my mother's solicitude, telling him that she would have done almost anything to find out what had happened to her son. He smiled and grew pensive. "You know," he said, "that was one of the few humanizing moments in the whole war for me, and I've cherished it ever since."

And a friendship was built on that anxious phone call from a concerned mother to a general in time of war . . .

I never expected my father to go gently into that last good-night. I expected him to "rage, rage against the dying of the light." He was a fiercely competitive man in athletics, and he did not give up easily. Yet when his anguish became too great, he simply withdrew from life and went into a solitary world that none could penetrate. He had known the best—of life and love and family— and leaving was the worst. He had nothing more to say, nothing more to do. His life and deeds had said it all, and everything was recorded in laughter and tears. There was nothing left but the waiting. And so he left us like a shadow into shade.

But my mother's silence was inspired by some cruel dementia, for she *did* have more to say. Her silence was unnatural. The silence of mothers—how loud it is, and how many echoes it sends down the corridors of time. And how long it lasts! A silence louder and longer than all of our tomorrows!

I remember one day in her ninety-ninth year when she recited eleven verses of Longfellow's *The Day Is Done*, and I can still hear her intoning the last stanza:

> *And the night shall be fill'd with music*
> *And the cares that infest the day,*

Shall fold their tents, like the Arabs,
And as silently steal away.

It was a poem she had memorized in the fourth grade and had won a prize for reciting in front of the class. She could also recite Tennyson, Shakespeare, and Gray's *Elegy*, as well as many others. There was so much to be said! In two or three lifetimes she couldn't have said it all.

Today, years after her leaving, how quiet it is, how heavy the silence. There are so many things I would still like to discuss with her—the why of things: the earthquakes that destroyed the basilica of Saint Francis of Assisi and took the lives of thousands in Turkey; the memoir *Angela's Ashes*; the monarch butterfly in her backyard and the problem of free will; this business of growing old and can there be good without God; even the other ten verses of Longfellow's poem that won her a prize as a little girl . . .

But mothers will always have the last word—memory will see to that!

There are only so many beads to a broken rosary. Before long the planting will be over, and it will be harvest time. The farmer has only so many years to sow and reap, and then it will be a time to rest. And there are only so many years of silence for all the dead mothers before the promise becomes a chorus and they are heard again.

Meeting at 35,000 Feet

AS Aviation Cadets in the Army Air Forces in World War II we were encouraged by both the times and our leaders to be religious and, if possible, to attend the services of our choice on Sundays. We were constantly being reminded that, as high-flying aviators we were among those closest to God, a kind of sanctity conferred by proximity. A case of nearer, my God, to Thee. Altitude was a wonderful and paradoxical reference: it had a way of both confusing and clarifying mysteries. And we cadets didn't have to be encouraged in the belief that we had God on our side and that our cause was just. I was to discover years later that the German *Luftwaffe* was told and came to believe the very same things. But those were times when moral colors were more black and white and less of gray.

Now, some 60 years later, I still feel a youthful exhilaration when I fly, even on commercial airliners. And, looking out over a silver wing and across a deck of blossoming clouds I am still willing to believe that I am in God's precincts and that God is still in His Heaven and all's right with the world, both above and beneath. But then, when our cruising altitude is reached, my reverie is interrupted by the more pedestrian sound of carts being pushed down the narrow aisle as "snacks" are offered to the passengers.

Sometimes, on commercial flights, I get the peculiar feeling that I am the only one who is aware of the miracles around us. I see others playing and working with computers, talking on telephones, sleeping or gripping their arm rests and staring straight ahead in some inner struggle for composure. And I remind myself that we are in a capsule, hurling through space at 600 miles an hour at an altitude of 35,000 feet. It seems, for most of the other passengers, miracle has turned to commonplace and I am the only one on the edge of discovery.

I look at my watch, set and checked for accuracy before take-off. It is 12:30 p.m. on February 17th in the year 2000. The ETA and date are important for I am meeting a living soul in 9 minutes—the soul of my Mother who died on that date four years before at 12:39 p.m. My anticipated meeting will be the closest I have come to her since her leaving.

Oh, I have visited the family grave many times. I have brought tears, flowers, prayers, memories and even a few regrets. But during my graveside visits I have always been painfully aware that the six-foot degree of separation was temporary. That, one day, I should see face-to-face. That, no matter what happened to the body, the soul would not be imprisoned in earth, that its destiny was flight. That, no longer bound by the laws of physics, we must look skyward to find another home and permanence of the spirit.

The meeting was not planned, yet it was no accident either. It just seemed to emerge from a confusion of schedules, computer print-outs and telephone conversations. From hastily-made dates, times, flight numbers and airports. And then, quite suddenly it was there—printed on a ticket like a surprising and joyful contract. And, as beneficiary, I felt like the latest Prince of Serendipity!

I would be airborne on the anniversary of her death, right down to the minute! No matter the weather below, the sun would be shining on our reunion. I could count on it. The clouds would be our red carpet to anticipation.

Her death had come shortly after St. Valentine's Day. She had been presented with a gift, a teddy bear, white, with a red ribbon around its neck and an over-sized Valentine heart. A teddy bear for kids, I had thought at the time, not for a woman of one hundred. And yet— I had seen in her and in other older people a kind of going-home syndrome, a return to childhood, taking again the long way home. And hadn't she told me more than once: "Nobody dies old." From the shadows of her dementia, she had spoken. Hadn't she kept in her "Book of Hope" a list of names of people and places, a map of the streets—all of her girlhood home? Hadn't she said a thousand times: "Well, I'd better be going home now"? And hadn't *home,* for her, come to mean her *childhood* home? Hadn't she kept alive a hope made of memories that rose phoenix-like from the ashes? A chart to shape the geography of home.

NOBODY DIES OLD! It is the child that dies again in all innocence and wonder.

We met, my Mother and I, at 12:39 p.m. somewhere in that airliner's wake on the way to San Antonio. I wish I could report seeing a vision; hearing her voice, but I cannot. And yet there are miracles to report, miracles of *feeling,* that vibrant awareness that something important was happening. Something beyond and outside myself and my poor powers to translate from the silence.

The sky, with its cloud sculpture and blinding sun formed the background against which the drama was played. It was a *feeling* more than anything else, a feeling that couldn't be defined: you couldn't say it, not in any language! You couldn't capture it in a phrase any more than you could throw a net of words around *love, hope* or *promise.* But there were *feelings,* seismic in the heart.

Intellect waited in the wings; knowledge did too, for they were merely intruders on this greater awareness. There were only feeling, intuition and the language of memory. It was a place where the past and the present came together like twins after a long absence, wordless, yet complete. Some braille that souls could touch!

Look into the sunset and then try to say it! Bite your tongue and then try to put the sensation into words! Time

seemed to stand still. Speed and distance hung in the balance. Past and present merged. Yes, there were miracles, miracles in disguise as they usually are. Miracles in the disguise
of the ordinary. And in that time and place I re-lived a day
when a boy and his mother stole a wealth of summers under
dogwood and lilacs. And the great revelation of that experience was that there were no ordinary days—every one was
as magical, as mysterious as sunrise and just as promising.

There were no ordinary days!

That was what I learned from that meeting at 35,000 feet.
That miracles happened in ordinary time. No, it is not a contradiction: *miracles* and *ordinary* may appear in the same sentence, as in the same life. For the mother-son bond is a strong
one: share the same heartbeat and you share most other
things including hopes, dreams, victories, defeats, even
deaths and entrances. And meetings at 35,000 feet. My
Mother, who was often my wing-person in life had asked me
near the end: "Fly me home?" And I had done it, this last
favor. In death, she became my lodestar . . .

Our humanity is in our feelings and our capacity to be
true to those feelings. I had to make the ascent to 35,000 feet
to find a backyard garden and an ordinary, yet miraculous,
afternoon that had made an enduring memory, more blessed
for the sharing.

"Nobody dies old," she had said. I had to meet her at
35,000 feet to appreciate that she was speaking of the miraculous birth. And to appreciate its joyful and redeeming corol-
lary: every ending is also a beginning.

An Open Letter to My Mother

DEAR Mom,

Today at Mass an infant girl was baptized. The priest, celebrating the Eucharist for the first time in this, his new parish, requested that each member of the congregation who was able come forward and make the Sign of the Cross on the infant's forehead. The idea, related to the gospel reading, was to involve the entire church community in the welcoming ceremony, a kind of "hands on" involvement designed to ". . . make a joyful noise unto the Lord." The intent was to make us all godparents again, to extend to us the privilege and the responsibility of sharing in a life beginning, now newly dedicated to God.

One by one we came forward and anointed her with the Sign of the Cross and, if I read those facial expressions correctly, with smiles, heart-felt wishes and silent prayers for a long and happy life. I noticed too that the steps of the older folk were lighter as they approached the altar and I do not doubt that many were remembering the time when they presented their own child to a welcoming crowd and to God. The young danced down the aisles toward the baby in an instant recognition of the joy inherent in the proceedings. And I couldn't help thinking that all that was needed to re-create a mid-summer's nativity scene were some shepherds, wise men and a few foreign royalty. Perhaps some gentle animals as well.

The proud mother held out her baby girl to the lines of people as though the infant were a flesh offering. "Take her and give her your blessing!" she seemed to be saying. There was joy in the mother's eyes—and a certain pleading as well, as though she was both challenged and afraid of what might be ahead for the child she had brought into the world. And there was a frightening innocence in the face of the infant as her tiny hands reached out to strangers, a vulnerability that made my heart turn over. But, all in all, it was a happy scene: one of rejoicing and celebration—all about a baby's starting out in life, carrying our future hopes with her as well as her own . . .

And Mother, listen. The strange part of it all was this: as I approached the baby I saw *you!* **Not as mother but as child!**

It was that old photograph in the family album, taken in the year of your birth, 1896. You were in Mama's arms, held out in the same offertory way, as if being presented to a waiting and adoring world. And in the very instant I bent over to make the Sign of the Cross on her forehead I felt you leave the grave and rise to glory! You left in mid-winter and now it is summer, your favorite time, and days now are green and blooming. And the feeling overwhelmed me that this was *your* second chance as well. And as this little stranger named Sarah lived, so too did you!

And just as suddenly this hole in my heart called *absence* was filled with your presence. As I came to that baby at the altar so I came to you—or you to me, I don't know which. But there was a blessing exchanged. A spiritual transfer took place between the Sarah of 100 days and the Ruth of 100 years! And for now Time had no dominion!

At the point in the ceremony in which Sarah's parents and godparents repeated her baptismal vows, the congregation joined in and renewed their own vows, one of which was to believe in the resurrection of the dead and the promise of life to come. And because of a baby named Sarah and a testament of shared memories I said aloud "Amen!"

It was you, Mother, who gave me my faith; mothered it over the years until it was able to stand on its own. It was you who introduced me to God in what often seemed a godless world. It was you who defined and refined all the virtues I know and may come to know. And this is my prayer *to* you and *for* you: that, like Sarah, and all the promises we made to her this day, your expectations, hopes, wishes and prayers have also come true and that a Lord's invitation: "Let the little children come unto me!" has included you once again.

I'll write again soon, Mom. There is so much I failed to say when I had the chance. But time is once more on our side: eternity is time enough. Remember Sister, me and the rest of the family. And remember Sarah, the baby girl, who led me back to you . . .

Your loving son.

An Eternal Reunion

I STOOD before my great-grandfather's grave for the first time, feeling the tides, historical and familial, take me back in time. And my thoughts suddenly came out as sound: "If it weren't for him and the rest, I wouldn't be here." The idea came as a shock to me: that the contents of this neglected grave and others like it in a neglected part of Northern New York could possibly have any connection with me in the here and now. But it was true. Along with others, I owed him for the gift of life.

My great-grandfather was one of a chain of people that stretched back into obscurity, perhaps all the way back to the savannas. And over the years the chain could have been broken at any point, and I would not now be here contemplating my own presence—and his. I wondered how many miracles must have happened to allow me to stand where I was standing, to think what I was thinking. How many crises of faith and survival? How many near misses? Yet here I was, and six feet or so beneath me, one of the towering dead, one of those responsible for the present.

The headstone was tilted, discolored, and porous, the writing difficult to read. I reached into my pocket and removed a sepia photograph in a small ornate frame and studied it. And it seemed as if there were an instant resurrection! The bones in the grave fleshed out, seemed to stir in becoming the young man in the picture, alive and somewhat solemn in the serious business of posing. A name had taken form and shape. History had encroached on the present.

I stood there for what must have been almost half an hour paying my respects and offering some random prayers for a soul that I was sure had survived what lay beneath, had risen to a greater glory. A soul that continued to grow in my imagination. A child, a boy-soldier in his country's cruelest war, a

husband, a father, a relative, an ancestor of future generations. So many things! He seemed so much greater than himself somehow!

Connections were made in that half-hour. We had never
met, he and I, and yet blood lines and blood truths united us.
We were strangers yet kinsmen. I got the feeling that if he
were to rise up like Lazarus, I should know him. We should
have things in common. There would be things to say. We
would be strangers, but strangers on the verge of discovery.
And I wondered how much of myself I was projecting into
that grave. How much of what he had become had been of
my invention, my creation, even my fiction?

I suddenly remembered an old woman in one of the rural
areas in Northern New York. She tended a family graveyard
behind her house. In summer the grave sites were always
mowed and trimmed and decorated with religious icons,
seasonal flowers, and small American flags. In winter there
was a shovel-wide path to each grave.

I heard the story from one of her distant relatives, who
gently accused her of having some benign form of dementia.
The old woman's husband, a merchant seaman, had been
lost at sea. Her son had been declared missing in action in
World War II. Her husband had become a part of the North
Atlantic, and her son was buried on some volcanic island in
the South Pacific. Continents apart. Yet, through an act of will
and her imagination, she had brought them together in their
own backyard, together and at the place called home. If not a
happy ending exactly, then at least a comforting one. Her
memory, her loyalty, and her enduring love had brought the
tragedy of loss to a closure. Two empty graves had been
filled by an old woman's love, her requiem . . .

I remember, too, the graves of Native Americans on the
open prairie of the American West. The graves were usually
marked with a scattering of colorful and "sacred" stones.

And in the absence of written records, graves were marked by memory. The survivors could tell the story of each of the dead, even down to the small humanizing touches that rounded out a life and resurrected a memory.

"This one was a great joker, don't you know. Like a boy he was and in a man's body, forever young at heart." And then an old woman, the keeper of memories, would tell a few stories to complete her portrait.

"Why stones?" I asked her once when I had been on the reservation for a short time.

She smiled, adjusting her dark umbrella to protect herself from the fierce sun. "The prairie is a place of wind and sun," she reminded me. "Flags would be blown away in no time, and flowers would be wilted before we got back home. Even plastic flowers would melt." And so she had placed stones on the grave—stones like crystal tears to mark a sorrow and a triumph.

"And in winter time?" I asked.

She was patient with me. "In winter *WakaNtaNka*, the Great Mystery, will watch over him. But God willing, I will be back with the blossoms of spring."

"And when you are gone?"

"The children already know this place. I have brought them here often. And later their children will know it. We do not write it down or draw maps. We keep it here!" She made a fist and struck her breast gently.

Her private genealogy: a record of the heart!

I remember, too, my own parents telling me that in the early years of this twentieth century, Sunday was not only church day but cemetery day. Many people went from church directly to the cemetery to bring the dead into the circle of the living. They brought flowers, memories, and prayers. They sat on benches and told stories of the dead. They mixed laughter and tears, dust and living flesh.

When I was old enough, I was included too. I remember being restless and anxious to salvage some playtime from a long Sunday. But I also remember being impressed by this celebration of absence, this triumph of the imagination! My mother told me that the living were the dead on holiday.

"Is great-grandfather on holiday?" I would ask.

"Yes, dear," she would answer quietly, "for as long as someone remembers. "

Holy days, holidays—days of grace and memory!

On the day I visited my great-grandfather, I visited other family grave sites as well—ancestors tucked away in remote corners of a country graveyard. Summer was the time for mixing life and death, for winter would bring folds of snow and the arctic chill of neglect. In late spring the place bloomed resurrection. So with my genealogy in hand and in the shade of the family tree, I took my pictures of stone angels and stone crosses. Later I made tracings of grave inscriptions after first brushing the moss from between the lettering. And in the reverie between life and distant death, I visited other places, other times . . . listened to other voices . . . sounded other depths . . .

There were a few other people in the cemetery that beautiful summer day, visitors who knew their way around and needed no maps or directions. Some sat on benches, while others sat on the grass and ate lunch out of paper bags. Sometimes there was the sudden ring of laughter and the soft words of remembrance. There was a quiet holiday atmosphere that hung over the place, a holiday that recognized no boundaries between worlds. There was only the distance of a breath between visitors and permanent residents.

A soprano voice rose in song: "Amazin' Grace." Sweet and low, the melody seemed to fill the summer day, a song woven into a tapestry.

It was a reunion, a family reunion that took place that midsummer day, a reunion of one member from earth and five members from their places in eternity. A gathering of kin and kind. Some had come from the greatest possible distances in time and space. Some had crossed boundaries and barriers; some had come from strange dimensions. Generations met across a field of remembrance. There were introductions . . . old acquaintances met again . . . an exchange of histories and twicetold tales. There was an empathy, a coming together. There were laughter and tears—laughter that rang like echoes in a canyon and tears from the earthly side—and conversations that took the form of prayer. The day had a certain dreamlike quality about it, a day imagined perhaps but not lived. And yet it was lived! It was a holiday in the oldest and best sense of the meaning of that word—*holy day,* a day consecrated, a benediction of a day.

Afterword: The Short Ride to Eternity

AT my request the long, black hearse pulled into the driveway of mother's home, there to wait a few minutes before resuming her short ride to eternity. Along the white picket fence that bordered the drive a few verdant spears poked through the February ice and snow, spears that in another few weeks would pierce the spring. The driveway's blooming was a sight both sad and elating: for its tender gardener, life on this earth had ended but spring would be re-born over and over, a cycle of nature as well as the promise of Christianity.

The hearse was too big for the narrow driveway, the tires crunching over the ice in protest. And I remembered thinking that only a few days earlier how the coffin had been too large for her diminutive frame, though not her journeying soul. We waited in the drive a few minutes and then were on our way, lights on in the cars that made up the short funeral procession.

On the way to Calvary Cemetery we passed the Grand Union where I used to take her grocery shopping. The place was vacant, only the memories stirring. I pictured the way she would drape herself on a shopping cart and how it gave her the instant mobility her legs could no longer provide.

"It's as though I have wheels," she would exult, one of her few compliments to technology as she cruised the aisles. But she was too short to reach the things on higher shelves and needed my help.

Riding behind the hearse I watched it almost hit a squirrel that couldn't make up its mind and I reacted to the narrow escape for mother too, who would not have added even a small creature to her own leaving. And through the car window I noticed what looked like a Valentine heart shaped by a billowing cloud. And I remembered that her death came three days after Valentine's Day.

At the cemetery the rust-colored, granite stone engraved with three names waited for its second member, Ruth A. Paige, 1896—, the final date waiting to be filled in. Then there was my own name and date of birth waiting to complete the family, not counting the sister pledged to the Connecticut soil and her family there, yet only a few degrees of separation away. But the family was already complete in love's strict dimension. And looking at the marker I felt a sudden warmth of permanence I had not known before, the same warmth that had come with my mother's words about the sharing of what she called "...the you in me." And the stone seemed to reassure me of permanence in a transitory world, even in a field of strangers.

Ceremony and ritual dictated the graveside proceedings, the ceremony and ritual that left us free to mourn rather than to consider. And then, quite suddenly it was over—a century of life closed like a book. The highway behind us was suddenly all traffic. The trail of a jet sliced the sky. The sights and sounds of life asserting itself again.

But there would be a time for solitude and silence: endings usually come in whispers.

Someone tugged on my arm and I turned away from the raw wound of earth and the bridges that were already burning between our worlds, twice removed . . . "Until we meet again," I said to myself. It was a hope, a wish, a prayer, a promise, a healing benediction like the rain that had begun to fall.

But there would come a time when that sad and rainy parting would be replaced by a living and happier memory created by my daughters, a kind of victory over absence and loss. For in a small section of Sandy's yard there is a flower garden with a hand-painted sign contributed by Judith, a sign proclaiming: MISSY'S GARDEN. Only a few miles from the place mother lies, it is a garden transplanted, a garden moved flower by flower. It is a garden that invites her great great-granddaughter Hannah, to chase a monarch butterfly among its blossoms. A garden celebrating continuing life. A garden of perennials following the seasons in their best imitation of forever.

Epitaph

The following epitaph was written by the author who was
suffering from a back injury at the time of his mother's funeral
and could not go to the lectern and deliver it himself.
Instead, it was read by her grandson, Jonathan Adams,
in the Church of Saint Thomas the Apostle in Delmar, New York.
Jon also sang "Amazing Grace" at the ceremony
of remembrance and celebration of her life.

ON behalf of our mother and family I would like to thank you for coming today. One of the difficulties of living to be 100 is that most of those you love, both family and friends, have gone on ahead without you.

My family, especially my daughters, will be relieved to know that I shall sing no sad songs at this ceremony, but rather regard it as a celebration of a life—a long and fulfilling life of love and dedication to family, God and her duty as she saw it. And although the family was the anchor to her life she made time for many others as well . . .

Our mother was born in 1896, the year William McKinely was elected president; the year RFD postal service was established; the year Mark Twain wrote his last major work; the year Ford assembled and road tested his famous automobile; the year gold was discovered in the Klondike; the year of the first modern Olympic games. All a very long time ago.

Our mother lived through two World Wars, wore out several rosaries praying first for her husband-to-be and then for her son. During WWII a dozen or more heroes called her "Ma" Paige and she was proud of that. Our home had long been a meeting place, a high school hang out and a bit like a USO canteen during the war years.

Our mother traveled infrequently and reluctantly: once she went to Los Angeles to bring home her dying mother. It must have been a sad, solitary and lonely journey, but was also an act of courage and devotion.

Our mother loved the springtime which was her own little experience with immortality. She loved flowers and growing things. I think her favorite place in the world was her own backyard.

She loved to read—and she was a writer of fragments and scraps that my sister and I have collected and preserved over the years. One of these that I discovered recently said: "We, the old, are people to whom something important is about to happen." There were other fragments equally as moving. I wish she had written more but conversation was more important to her than putting things down on paper. I credit her with teaching her son to see beneath the surface of things and to record his findings.

Our mother had a good life: she had 95 good years and five lesser years. The bad years will always sit like an anvil on our hearts but they will not crowd out the good years from our memory. It would be wrong to let that happen.

In November, 1995 my mother was in St. Peter's Hospital with pneumonia and one day, while my daughter, Judith, and I were visiting, she woke up from one of her naps, sat up in her reclining chair and asked: "Harry, will you fly me home?"

Judith and I were startled by her question that came like lightning from a clear sky. We were even more astonished because never had my mother flown and I had not piloted an aircraft for a long time.

But I told her yes, I *would* fly her home.

Her question, which we thought might have been inspired by her fever or dementia, has proved to be prophetic, even insightful, for I am flying her home now, this very day.

Death puts life in a perspective: that is why it is necessary perhaps. We might not be as alive if we did not face the prospect of death. But our faith, her faith, teaches us that in endings there are also beginnings. And I am sure she is ready, even anxious, to begin all over again.

Some say that when we die someone we love will be waiting on the other side to help us across. With our mother it could be Monte, her beloved Mama, Margaret or longtime friend and neighbor, Henry MacMillan. I hope they are all there to greet her. And may the living breath of our prayers also find her and be with her always.

Additional Titles Published by Resurrection Press, a Catholic Book Publishing Imprint

A Rachel Rosary *Larry Kupferman*	$4.50
A Season in the South *Marci Alborghetti*	$10.95
And A Child Will Lead *Anita Constance, S.C.*	$7.95
Blessings All Around *Dolores Leckey*	$8.95
Catholic Is Wonderful *Mitch Finley*	$4.95
Come, Celebrate Jesus! *Francis X. Gaeta*	$4.95
Days of Intense Emotion *Keeler/Moses*	$12.95
Feasts of Life *Jim Vlaun*	$12.95
From Holy Hour to Happy Hour *Francis X. Gaeta*	$7.95
Grace Notes *Lorraine Murray*	$9.95
Healing through the Mass *Robert DeGrandis, SSJ*	$9.95
Our Grounds for Hope *Fulton J. Sheen*	$7.95
The Healing Rosary *Mike D.*	$5.95
Healing Your Grief *Ruthann Williams, OP*	$7.95
Heart Peace *Adolfo Quezada*	$9.95
Life, Love and Laughter *Jim Vlaun*	$7.95
The Joy of Being an Altar Server *Joseph Champlin*	$5.95
The Joy of Being a Catechist *Gloria Durka*	$4.95
The Joy of Being a Eucharistic Minister *Mitch Finley*	$5.95
The Joy of Being a Lector *Mitch Finley*	$5.95
The Joy of Being an Usher *Gretchen Hailer, RSHM*	$5.95
The Joy of Marriage Preparation *McDonough/Marinelli*	$5.95
The Joy of Music Ministry *J.M. Talbot*	$6.95
The Joy of Preaching *Rod Damico*	$6.95
The Joy of Praying the Rosary *James McNamara*	$5.95
The Joy of Teaching *Joanmarie Smith*	$5.95
The Joy of Worshiping Together *Rod Damico*	$5.95
Lights in the Darkness *Ave Clark, O.P.*	$8.95
Loving Yourself for God's Sake *Adolfo Quezada*	$5.95
Meditations for Survivors of Suicide *Joni Woelfel*	$8.95
Mother Teresa *Eugene Palumbo, S.D.B.*	$5.95
Mourning Sickness *Keith Smith*	$8.95
Personally Speaking *Jim Lisante*	$8.95
Practicing the Prayer of Presence *Muto/van Kaam*	$8.95
Prayers from a Seasoned Heart *Joanne Decker*	$8.95
Praying the Lord's Prayer with Mary *Muto/vanKaam*	$8.95
5-Minute Miracles *Linda Schubert*	$4.95
Sabbath Moments *Adolfo Quezada*	$6.95
Season of New Beginnings *Mitch Finley*	$4.95
Season of Promises *Mitch Finley*	$4.95
Sometimes I Haven't Got a Prayer *Mary Sherry*	$8.95
St. Katharine Drexel *Daniel McSheffery*	$12.95
Stay with Us *John Mullin, SJ*	$3.95
What He Did for Love *Francis X. Gaeta*	$5.95
Woman Soul *Pat Duffy, OP*	$7.95
You Are My Beloved *Mitch Finley*	$10.95

For a free catalog call 1-800-892-6657
www.catholicbookpublishing.com